THE CRITICS

General Editor

The Critics Debate
General Editor Michael Scott
Published titles:
Sons and Lovers Geoffrey Harvey
Bleak House Jeremy Hawthorn
The Canterbury Tales Alcuin Blamires
Tess of the d'Urbervilles Terence Wright
The Waste Land and Ash Wednesday Arnold P. Hinchliffe
Paradise Lost Margarita Stocker
King Lear Ann Thompson
Othello Peter Davison
The Winter's Tale Bill Overton
Gulliver's Travels Brian Tippett
Blake: Songs of Innocence and Experience David Lindsay
Measure for Measure T. F. Wharton
Hamlet Michael Hattaway
The Tempest David Daniell
Coriolanus Bruce King
Wuthering Heights Peter Miles
The Metaphysical Poets Donald Mackenzie
The Great Gatsby Stephen Matterson
To the Lighthouse Su Reid

Further titles are in preparation

TO THE LIGHTHOUSE

Su Reid

© Su Reid 1991

All rights reserved. No reproduction, copy or transmission
of this publication may be made without written permission.

No paragraph of this publication may be reproduced, copied
or transmitted save with written permission or in accordance
with the provisions of the Copyright, Designs and Patents Act
1988 or under the terms of any licence permitting limited
copying issued by the Copyright Licensing Agency,
33–4 Alfred Place, London WC1E 7DP.

Any person who does any unauthorised act in relation to
this publication may be liable to criminal prosecution and
civil claims for damages.

First Published 1991

Published by
MACMILLAN EDUCATION LTD
Houndmills, Basingstoke, Hampshire RG21 2XS
and London
Companies and representatives
throughout the world

Typeset by LBJ Enterprises Ltd
Chilcompton and Tadley

Printed in Hong Kong

British Library Cataloguing in Publication Data
   To the Lighthouse.—(The critics debate).
   Reid, Su
   1. Fiction in English. Woolf, Virginia, 1882–1941
   I. Title II. Series
   823.912

ISBN 0–333–47386–8
ISBN 0–333–47387–6 pbk

For George, Jane, Alison, and Benet, with love and thanks

Contents

Acknowledgements 6
General Editor's Preface 7

Part One: Survey

A 'Difficult' Text

Early Reviews 9
Virginia Woolf's Discussion of Modern Novels 10
'What Does She Mean?': Criticism in Woolf's Lifetime 14
'Where Does She Fit In?': Virginia Woolf in Literary Histories 18

A 'Structured' Text

New Criticism and its Followers: Symbolic and Allegorical Readings 25
Mythological and Freudian Readings 33
Readings in Aesthetic Theory 38
The Narrative Voice 43

A 'Feminist' Text

Virginia Woolf and Feminism 52
Biographical Readings 55
Theories of Femininity 65

Part Two: Appraisal of the Text

Attempts to Construct a Feminist Reading

Mrs Ramsay's Story 80
Disintegration of Self 85
The Narrative Voice Again 93

Bibliography 99
Index 113

Acknowledgements

I acknowledge with gratitude the permission given by the Executors of the Virginia Woolf Estate and the Hogarth Press for me to quote from *To the Lighthouse, A Room of One's Own, The Common Reader,* Volume III of *The Letters of Virginia Woolf,* edited by Nigel Nicolson and Joanne Trautmann, and Volume III of *The Essays of Virginia Woolf,* edited by Andrew McNeillie.

I wish to thank my colleagues and students at Teesside Polytechnic for their help and encouragement, especially Alma Cuthbertson, David R. Taylor, Ruth Whittaker, and Crispin Yelland for his knowledge of linguistic criticism; and the members of the Northern Network Seminars for their exciting meetings each term; and Flora Alexander for her encouragement over many years; and Sandra Tait and, above all, my family for their patience.

Su Reid

General Editor's Preface

OVER THE last few years the practice of literary criticism has become hotly debated. Methods developed earlier in the century and before have been attacked and the word 'crisis' has been drawn upon to describe the present condition of English Studies. That such a debate is taking place is a sign of the subject discipline's health. Some would hold that the situation necessitates a radical alternative approach which naturally implies a 'crisis situation'. Others would respond that to employ such terms is to precipitate or construct a false position. The debate continues but it is not the first. 'New Criticism' acquired its title because it attempted something fresh, calling into question certain practices of the past. Yet the practices it attacked were not entirely lost or negated by the new critics. One factor becomes clear: English Studies is a pluralistic discipline.

What are students coming to advanced work in English for the first time to make of all this debate and controversy? They are in danger of being overwhelmed by the cross-currents of critical approaches as they take up their study of literature. The purpose of this series is to help delineate various critical approaches to specific literary texts. Its authors are from a variety of critical schools and have approached their task in a flexible manner. Their aim is to help the reader come to terms with the variety of criticism and to introduce him or her to further reading on the subject and to a fuller evaluation of a particular text by illustrating the way it had been approached in a number of contexts. In the first part of the book a critical survey is given of some of the major ways the text has been appraised. This is done sometimes in a thematic manner, sometimes according to various 'schools' or 'approaches'. In the second part the authors provide their own appraisals of the text from their stated critical standpoint, allowing the reader the knowledge of their own particular approaches from which their views may in turn be evaluated. The series therein hopes to introduce and to elucidate criticism of authors and texts being studied and to encourage participation as the critics debate.

Michael Scott

PART ONE
SURVEY
A 'Difficult' Text

Early Reviews

Many students, and many critics, have admitted to finding Virginia Woolf's fiction difficult to read. The reason for this is quite clear in the first reviews of *To the Lighthouse*, anthologised in Beja's *Casebook* (1970) and in Majumdar and McLaurin's *Virginia Woolf: The Critical Heritage* (1975). Repeatedly, the reviewers comment on the novel's unfamiliar form, and decide it must represent an attempt to portray aspects of life not normally portrayed in novels.

The anonymous *Times Literary Supplement* review (Beja, 1970, pp. 73–6; Majumdar and McLaurin, 1975, pp. 193–5) praises the novel's design, but says it has no plot and its characters are indistinct. It supposes the real subject must therefore be abstract, perhaps to do with a meaning underlying events. The other review quoted in both anthologies, the American Conrad Aiken's from *Dial* (Beja, 1970, pp. 76–80; Majumdar and McLaurin, 1975, pp. 205–8), confesses irritation with the technical complexity, but then praises the form as a better-than-usual way of representing rather regrettably old-fashioned life and values.

Three reviews quoted only in *The Critical Heritage* similarly see the form as a way of representing something abstract. Kronenberger (pp. 195–8) and Edwin Muir (pp. 209–10) especially praise 'Time Passes' for its poetic representation of time; and Orlo Williams (pp. 201–5) discusses all Woolf's novels so far as attempts to embody her own personal vision, thinks this can be better achieved in poetry than in novels, but also thinks *To the Lighthouse*, being unlike a novel with a story, comes near to it.

Two assumptions dominate these reviews. One is the belief that any novel portrays, represents, things that exist outside it, that even existed before it was written. The other is the idea that the form and style of a novel are designed by the novelist to give the best possible representation of those things the novel is 'about'.

To the Lighthouse appeared unusual in its form. The reviewers therefore assumed that it was not representing usual things, that its overt account of family life couldn't really be the point. They posited something more abstract as the object of representation, though they varied as to what that abstract might be.

Any reader who makes the same assumptions immediately makes the novel seem difficult. This is partly because the 'meaning' of the novel is defined as elusive, as non-obvious. But it is also because the real interest of the reader is at once repressed. That interest is the actual experience of reading an unusual, a surprising, novel. But the attention is turned away from the experience of reading and towards an elusive goal, the attainment of a clear and fixed interpretation. What happens to the reader while reading is buried beneath the effort to label the novel correctly.

Virginia Woolf's Discussion of Modern Novels

These same assumptions, and their attendant difficulties, have dominated much discussion of *To the Lighthouse* until quite recently. They are unfortunately reinforced by some of Virginia Woolf's own critical essays.

Virginia Woolf was as famous as an essayist as she was as a novelist when *To the Lighthouse* was published in 1927. Two essays, *Mr Bennett and Mrs Brown*, published in 1924, and 'Modern Fiction' published in her collection of essays *The Common Reader* in 1925, have repeatedly been cited as manifestos for her generation of novelists. Taken together, they are seen to proclaim a confrontation between the modernists, or 'Georgians', and the 'Edwardians', represented by Bennett, Galsworthy, and Wells, and to accuse the latter of failing to represent 'life' adequately. On the basis of this, and of the assumption that her novels' unfamiliar designs are intended somehow to portray deeper truths about life, Virginia Woolf has become a critical icon. To this icon is attached the desire of many critics to reduce complex novels to a single definite meaning. If modernist fiction is trying to represent 'life' more fully, more truly, the assumption goes, then it is the reader's task to unravel the text and define the 'life' it is talking about.

A careful reading of these essays, however, reveals a more complex situation. Both essays went through various processes before reaching their familiar forms, and these processes involve the abandonment of a struggle by Woolf to try to articulate a much more radical idea.

The essays are about the experience of writing, not of reading, novels. Their complaints about Bennett, Wells and Galsworthy are based on anxieties about them as models for younger novelists, and are not attacks on them as bad novelists from a reader's point of view. 'Modern Fiction' is actually a revised version of an earlier article 'Modern Novels', written for the *Times Literary Supplement* in 1919 (McNeillie, 1988, pp. 30–7). The earlier version does not include the famous 'Life is not a series of gig-lamps symmetrically arranged' (McNeillie, 1984, p. 150), and it is a better essay than its later version, more consistently argued. The difference is that this earlier version is concerned with the novelist's difficulty in finding the means of articulating his or her own rapidity and variety of thought and perception; whereas in the later version the attention has been shifted on to an idea about portraying variety of thought and perception in the characters, with the novelist now apparently thought of as a distanced observer of all this. The earlier version says

> Is it not possible that . . . if one were free and could set down what one chose, there would be no plot, little probability, and a vague general confusion in which the clear-cut features of the tragic, the comic, the passionate, and the lyrical were dissolved beyond the possibility of separate recognition? The mind, exposed to the ordinary course of life, receives upon its surface a myriad impressions – trivial, fantastic, evanescent, or engraved with the sharpness of steel. From all

sides they come, an incessant shower of innumerable atoms, composing in their sum what we might venture to call life itself; and to figure further as the semi-transparent envelope, or luminous halo, surrounding us from the beginning of consciousness to the end. (McNeillie, 1988, p. 33)

It is the diversity of experience in the novelist's mind that is discussed here. But in the later version the novelist is construed as someone who can watch this process from a position of stability and power; 'Examine for a moment an ordinary mind on an ordinary day. The mind receives a myriad impressions' (McNeillie, 1984, pp. 149–50).

In between the two versions of this essay came *Mr Bennett and Mrs Brown*, originally entitled 'Character in Fiction' (McNeillie, 1988, pp. 420–38). This focuses directly on the question of how to represent a character, Mrs Brown. Although the observer of Mrs Brown is herself represented as a changing character within the story that opens this essay, the main concern is clearly with the need to develop a technique to represent the diversity of Mrs Brown from the position of an unproblematised observer.

This essay is the high point of a long-running dispute in print between Virginia Woolf and Arnold Bennett, the full details of which are not relevant here (but see Bibliography). What is relevant is that in this dispute Virginia Woolf largely abandoned, for the time being, her attempt to discuss novels in terms of representing the mind of the author, the perceiver. In December 1923 she had published a different, much shorter, essay under the same title of 'Mr Bennett and Mrs Brown' in *Nation and Athenaeum*, of which her husband Leonard was the literary editor. This essay (McNeillie, 1988, pp. 384–9; Majumdar and McLaurin, 1975, pp. 115–19) referred to an article by Arnold Bennett about younger novelists which, nine months earlier, had cited her *Jacob's Room* as an example of a praiseworthy novel which had the flaw of lacking memorable characters (Majumdar and McLaurin, 1975, pp. 112–14). It agreed with Bennett that characters are important in novels, and defended the younger novelists as attempting to find new ways of portraying them: the Georgians, she said, were in pursuit of their Mrs Brown and would one day manage to catch her. This essay was the first of a series about characters in fiction which Leonard ran for several months (Majumdar and McLaurin, 1975, pp. 115–32), and it made Virginia Woolf into a public representative of a supposed new way of portraying characters, thought of as existing independently and waiting to be properly captured.

Rachel Bowlby has discussed the later *Mr Bennett and Mrs Brown* as articulating a problem understood by feminists, the difficulty of representing female characters within a literary tradition that offers a limited range of images of women (Bowlby, 1988, pp. 7–11); and Makiko Minow-Pinkney has convincingly argued that in 'Modern Novels' and its later version Virginia Woolf has disguised under a dispute about how her generation should write novels, another dispute that really surfaced only with *A Room of One's Own* in 1929 (Minow-Pinkney, 1987, pp. 1–23). There Woolf describes the problems of women writers trying to express their own consciousness within a male-dominated literary tradition that embodies different ways of thinking. These are helpful readings, but they do not quite take account of the shift within these essays. The shift is towards a conventional view of the author as observer of 'life', and away from something much more problematic. Perhaps if Woolf had had available to her the concept of the narrative voice as a construct itself, and as different from the author, she would not so easily have capitulated to the idea of novels as the observing author's representations of characters. However that might be, the revised version, 'Modern Fiction', assumes that a novel represents its characters, who are somewhere waiting to be represented, and who are largely separate from the unproblematised voice that tells us about them.

We have many more critical theories available to us than Virginia Woolf had, and changes in the way *To the Lighthouse* has been read demonstrate an increasing interest in the issues so tentatively suggested by 'Modern Novels'. But it is also true that readings of the novel have been hampered by the continuance of the idea that its author is a detached observer who uses different tools to represent something outside the novel accurately, and who appears as narrator in the novel; and also that a reader is merely an observer of the resulting text. It is true, too, that Virginia Woolf's essays have been cited in support of these hampering suppositions.

'What Does She Mean?': Criticism in Woolf's Lifetime

In the period between the publication of *To the Lighthouse* and Virginia Woolf's death in 1941, critical discussion of her work only compounded the problems I have described. Puzzlement about the forms of the novels often still led readers to look for a separate 'meaning' that would label and explain them, or to complain when no such 'meaning' appeared.

Some critics, wishing perhaps to avoid condemning the novels, offered another idea, suggesting that they were highly structured in formal aesthetic patterns with little reference to 'life'. In 1932 Winifred Holtby, in the first full-length book about Virginia Woolf, discussed the unity built up in *To the Lighthouse* by the way episodes echo earlier episodes (pp. 144–7). In the same year Q. D. Leavis in *Fiction and the Reading Public* called it beautifully constructed although difficult to read (1932, p. 223). In 1934 John Hawley Roberts described Woolf as wanting to portray characters only in terms of their place in an abstract pattern or design (Roberts, 1934, p. 589).

But these suggestions are always made against the background of an expectation that novels should contain a detachable representation of and comment about life.

The self-regarding journal *Scrutiny* carried a hostile essay by M. C. Bradbrook in its first number in May 1932. Its main complaint is that Virginia Woolf is competent at portraying single moments, but is unable to combine these into a coherent structure; and that she cannot so combine them because she lacks a set of moral values in terms of which each event or moment might be given a significance in relation to the others and might become part of a rational discussion of life. This essay famously accuses Virginia Woolf of deliberately avoiding serious thought (Bradbrook, 1932, p. 38). Clearly Bradbrook herself has found the form of the novel puzzling, but has attributed this to a supposed lack of organisation and meaning *within the text*.

Even Woolf's friend E. M. Forster said something similar. In 1925 he had praised her early novels for their representation of moments and details, but had hoped her later work would go on to discover how to link these together into consistent characters to form, simultaneously, a new kind of structure and a memorable representation of life (Forster, 1936, pp. 127–8). Still unsatisfied in 1927, he wrote of her in *Aspects of the Novel* as a fantasist avoiding sustained and coherent thought about the objects she described (Forster, 1927, pp. 26–7). Even in his obituary Rede Lecture in 1941 he still regretted that the detailed items of her work did not relate to each other coherently and memorably (Forster, 1951, pp. 256–7).

In this lecture Forster begins to resort to the idea of an aesthetic rather than a representational unity, and goes on to suggest that her novels have the merits, not of fiction which should say something memorable about life outside itself, but of poetry (Forster, 1951, p. 267). The comparison with poetry had become quite common. Robert Peel had also seen in the novels an absence of coherent philosophical ideas about the world and a presence, instead, of poetry, which he thought inappropriate in novels (Peel, 1933, pp. 78–9). Elizabeth Monroe praised *To the Lighthouse* above Woolf's other novels because of its closeness to poetry (Monroe, 1940, p. 220). The assumption seems to be that poetry is a medium possessing decorative and complex forms which do not refer to anything outside themselves.

Other critics, however, tried to impose a comment about life, a meaning, on the novel even while discussing its 'poetry'. Harold Nicolson, in *The Listener* in 1931, had called Virginia Woolf a lyric poet who had become a novelist accidentally, and further went on to advise readers of this difficult fiction to read without familiar expectations, and to allow their minds to accept impressions gradually. He nevertheless went on to define a central theme in *To the Lighthouse* – that of mutability in human affairs. In the same year William Empson had also used the idea of a poetic use of language when discussing the difficulty of fitting the echoing details of *To the Lighthouse* into coherent and memorable messages; but he had wished for an annotated edition, or an index, to help him fit the details and their meanings clearly together (pp. 207–8, 216). In 1934 Peter Burra described Mrs Woolf as a poet who had eliminated plot (p. 114), but also wished for an interpreter so that her mind could be clearly understood (p. 113). The assumption is that a reader may read poetry in order to perceive the details of its form, but will read fiction in order to be given judgements about life. Fictional texts which do not immediately provide such judgements are regarded as improper poetic novels and as needing to have meanings forced upon them, if necessary by an annotated edition or an interpreter.

The critics of this period suggested various readings which served to force a meaning on to *To the Lighthouse*, and in doing so they set ways of trying to read the novel which have persisted into recent times. Empson's reading, requesting an index, makes the novel into a series of symbols of which the most important is the lighthouse itself, symbolising human energy and aspiration (p. 205). Burra saw the lighthouse as a symbol of the different visions of the characters within the book (p. 123). J. H. Roberts described both Mrs Ramsay and the lighthouse as symbols of abstract reality rather than as direct representations of a person or an object (Roberts, 1934, p. 596). These readings enable the critics to reassure themselves that the novel is clearly about life beyond itself even although it is not describing that life in a familiar way. They do, however, indicate that a reader should not try to see the novel as a description of the domestic life it might seem to represent; they label the novel as complex, as difficult, and as somehow abstract.

The same is true of readings which argue about the relationship of Woolf's work to academic philosophy, and especially to the work of the French philosopher Henri Bergson. Critics using this notion are vague as to what Bergson actually wrote, but they seize upon reference to him as a way of explaining Woolf's work. The most famous example is William Troy's 'Virginia Woolf and the Novel of Sensibility', published in 1932 and quoted in Beja's *Casebook* (Beja, 1970, pp. 85–9). Troy indicates that even if Mrs Woolf had not read Bergson she must be influenced by him through the writings of contemporaries, and that she had learned from such sources to try to write about, to represent, only subjective perceptions rather than objective observations. This argument, which represents Bergson as saying that the perceiving mind is more real than the things it perceives (Beja, 1970, pp. 85–6), actually allows Troy to think that in fact life and things do exist objectively, ready to be perceived, but that Virginia Woolf tries to represent something else.

In 1934 Roberts related Bergson and Proust to the theme he imposed on *Mrs Dalloway* and *To the Lighthouse*, namely an attempt to differentiate between clock-time and the individual's consciousness of time through memory (Roberts, 1934, p. 596). In 1940 Monroe also related what she described as Woolf's experiments about time to contemporary developments in science, especially the theory of relativity and Bergsonian theories of the unconscious (pp. 221–2), and argued that Woolf's intention was to represent sensibility, apparently thinking of that as an object. Winifred Holtby's *Virginia Woolf* had referred to a French critic, M. Florio Delattre, whose recent *Le Roman Psychologique de Virginia Woolf* had, Holtby said, suggested a connection between Bergson, Proust, Joyce, and Woolf (Holtby, 1932, pp. 20–1). Holtby actually denies a direct connection between Bergson and Woolf, but she nevertheless uses the suggestion to impose an objective philosophical meaning on to Woolf's fiction, which she also sees as trying to represent the workings of the mind (pp. 21–2).

In these arguments the fiction is thus defined as 'about' something, but as difficult; and the readers are now defined as people who might, if possessed of the requisite learning, be able to observe the meaning from their own knowledgeable position outside the text.

The same is often true of arguments that assert that Virginia Woolf does, as 'Modern Fiction' is thought to suggest, represent the 'stream of consciousness' of some of her characters. Early examples of the use of this phrase were an article by E. W. Hawkins and a chapter in a book by P. Edgar, both of which use it as title. After Woolf's death many critics adopted it in discussions of her work. It is not a helpful idea. It prolongs the assumption that a novel is significant because of the things it describes, and it entirely obscures any interest either in the novel's narrative voice or in the experience of the reader while reading.

Apparently much simpler proposed readings that see *To the Lighthouse* as disguised autobiography reinforce the same assumptions. Raymond Mortimer, for example, praised *To the Lighthouse* solely for its portrayal of Woolf's father, Sir Leslie Stephen, in 1929. In January 1942, almost a year after Woolf's death, the chief guru of *Scrutiny*, F. R. Leavis, mounted a valedictory attack. He cited 'Modern Fiction' as proof that Virginia Woolf wanted her novels to be about life, to represent the impressions of the mind, and he, like Bradbrook, complained that those impressions are valueless unless they are part of a structured moral belief about the world (F. R. Leavis, 1942, pp. 295–7). However, he praised *To the Lighthouse*; that was because he too saw it as a representation of Sir Leslie Stephen. He therefore claimed that this novel alone is about life (p. 297). Critics have continued to impose knowledge of Virginia Woolf's life, derived from other texts, on to *To the Lighthouse* ever since. In doing this they are forcing a fixed interpretation derived from outside information on to the text of the novel.

In 1937 Herbert J. Muller's two versions of his essay 'Virginia Woolf and Feminine Fiction' offered an overview of Woolf's significance. Muller declared himself not an admirer of her work, which he considered genteel and bloodless; but he also considered it important in literary history for having abolished plot and story in order the better to represent the experience of life. His views summarise those developed during her lifetime, which formed the basis of many subsequent readings.

'Where Does She Fit In?': Virginia Woolf in Literary Histories

In 1953 Erich Auerbach's *Mimesis* was published in English. This is a major study of the techniques whereby that which is thought of as reality has been represented in European literature, starting with the Greeks and the Old Testament. Its final chapter, entitled 'The Brown Stocking', discusses modern techniques largely in terms of the fifth section of

'The Window', Part I of *To the Lighthouse*. It established Woolf as a very significant modernist writer, and it did so by discussion of a novel, not by quoting her essays.

This fascinating close reading of the passage in which Mrs Ramsay measures the stocking she is knitting against James's leg, in which Mrs Ramsay's thoughts range over her domestic responsibilities, and in which the narrator's thoughts range over other people's ideas about Mrs Ramsay, is important in two ways. It is important because it introduces the idea of the narrative voice as a distinct construct into discussion of the novel, and it is important because of the way it defines the phenomenon of modernism.

Auerbach compares the two parentheses, or digressions, that interrupt the description of the present action, the measuring of the stocking. The first (*TtL*, pp. 29–31) describes Mrs Ramsay's own thoughts, which are known to the narrator. In the second (*TtL*, pp. 31–2), however, someone more distanced appears to observe Mrs Ramsay, to ask questions about her which cannot be answered, to quote what other people have said about her, and to remember what her friend William Bankes has thought about her on a specific occasion in the past. Auerbach asks who this someone is. He assumes it is Virginia Woolf, but says that Virginia Woolf does not behave here like an author who has invented, and therefore knows all about, the characters. He refers to the author as male, which suggests an inexplicit assumption that the 'author' in the text is different from the person of the writer (Auerbach, 1953, p. 469). The idea of the narrative voice as a construct is introduced.

Auerbach then argues that in this second parenthesis the familiar knowledgeable narrator has disappeared; and that there exists, in this modern text, no source of information about the character of Mrs Ramsay except those within the novel itself, the other characters; there is no authoritative truth about her (1953, pp. 471–2). Modernism begins to be described as writing which undercuts the familiar construction of a single authoritative author/narrator telling the truth about his characters' lives.

At this point Auerbach seems after all to reassert the idea that the material of the novel exists independently of the text. He describes the assembling of different views of Mrs Ramsay – her own, the narrator's, Bankes's, others' – as attempts to achieve a more objective knowledge than that of one fixed observer (pp. 473–4). But then he proposes a much more radical idea: that this manner of narration, with its digressions and its recalling of diverse pieces of information, is itself exploring the workings of consciousness; that insignificant domestic events trigger sequences of ideas and thoughts which are themselves much more important to the person thinking them, to the narrative voice here, than the original domestic event (pp. 474–8). This idea, explained in terms of a reading of part of a novel, is surely close to what Virginia Woolf was beginning to say in her 1919 'Modern Novels': that a novel might not so much observe as demonstrate the workings of the mind.

With this reading Virginia Woolf was established as a major modernist, and *To the Lighthouse* as a major modernist text. Since then Virginia Woolf's work has been used in some English attempts to define modernism, especially by Malcolm Bradbury and David Lodge. These critics, however, still rely quite strongly on ideas about her generated in the 1930s, and especially the idea that her fiction is remote from experience, and poetic. This assumption dominates their ideas about modernism.

In his *Possibilities* in 1973 Bradbury cited Auerbach as establishing *To the Lighthouse* as a supreme example of modernism, a text that disposes of an objective narrator in favour of the representation of subjective consciousness and the randomness of events (Bradbury, 1973, pp. 121–2). But he then proceeds to produce an account of Woolf's work which defines modernism simply as a kind of writing that uses lyrical and symbolic techniques to indicate things not directly described. He discusses the idea of 'stream of consciousness' in some detail, referring it back to William James's *Principles of Psychology* (1890), which argued that reality exists only as it is created in consciousness (Bradbury, 1973, pp. 122–3), and on to ideas about the importance of moments of heightened consciousness, which he attributes to Woolf's Bloomsbury friends (pp. 123–5). He then describes modernist novels as representing the complex consciousness of their authors, as doing so by using pattern and lyricism and remote symbols, and as simultaneously indicating the impossibility of rational representation (pp. 125–33). His argument is still that the complexities of consciousness can be represented, with difficulty but objectively. He posits the existence of the author as a detached observer.

In his influential *The Modes of Modern Writing* (1977) David Lodge uses 'Modern Fiction', which he dates 1919, to begin to define modernist fiction; he, too, sees this as fiction using particular techniques in order to represent the human mind (pp. 44–6). Later in his book he introduces some of Woolf's novels as exemplifying his main thesis, that modernist fiction offers a predominantly metaphoric representation of experience, as contrasted with the predominantly metonymic representation of realist fiction (pp. 177–88). But much of his discussion of these novels is concerned with imposing a closed theme on them, a theme which he defines in terms of Lily's question at the start of 'The Lighthouse', Part III of *To the Lighthouse*, 'What does it mean, then, what can it all mean?' (*TtL*, p. 137). He sees the novels as asking that question and as demonstrating its futility even while, with their intricate forms, they keep the reader looking for an answer (pp. 177–80). His argument is intriguing, but it still assumes the novels can be thought of detachedly as offering an organised and closed image of consciousness, and also assumes that their meanings are remote from material experience.

It has perhaps become a common assumption in Britain that modernism was simply a series of experiments in representation. Certainly a recent author, Brian McHale, bases his *Postmodernist Fiction* (1987) on a defining contrast which states that modernist fiction was, indeed, primarily concerned only with ways in which we know or perceive the objective world, the existence of which was not itself considered problematic (McHale, 1987, pp. 9–11). This view of modernism seems to me to be the product of uninspected assumptions rather than of careful thought about those texts which have been labelled modernist; and perhaps to have missed the most radical part of Auerbach's discussion of *To the Lighthouse*, which suggests that modernist writing undercuts the very notion of objective representation.

Having labelled her as a modernist, histories and broadly based surveys of English Literature written since the Second World War have frequently marginalised the work of Virginia Woolf. They have perpetuated the idea of it as difficult and as avoiding discussion of important issues and experiences.

In *The English Novel* in 1954 Walter Allen described Woolf as possessing a small talent, while citing 'Modern Fiction', whose title he misquoted, as indicating her dedication to writing about a 'stream of consciousness'. He judged that she does this less successfully than some contemporaries, dismissed her as working within very narrow and female limitations, and discussed *To the Lighthouse* as symbolic prose-poetry (pp. 343–51). He repeated these views, in some of the same words, in his *Tradition and Dream* in 1964 (pp. 41–5).

F. W. Bradbrook's 1961 essay in Boris Ford's *The Pelican Guide to English Literature*, after complaining of stridency in *A Room of One's Own* and *Three Guineas*, described *To the Lighthouse* as combining autobiography with a poetic and symbolic method, so making its themes – time, beauty, art, absence, death – eternal rather than specific (in Ford, 1961, p. 265). So the novel is made to seem remote from experienced life, although Bradbrook quotes some of Woolf's essays to indicate she was trying to re-create life's complexities (in Ford, 1961, pp. 259–67). This essay was reproduced in Ford's *The New Pelican Guide* in 1983.

Even in Malcolm Bradbury's and James McFarlane's collection of essays in *Modernism* in 1976, Woolf appears only sporadically, when received ideas about her work fit easily into the various authors' ideas about modernism. Lily's picture is referred to by the editors as an archetype of art seeking harmony within itself rather than in life (p. 25); Woolf's novels are referred to by John Fletcher and Bradbury as having pattern rather than plot (p. 408); Melvin J. Friedman compares *The Waves* at some length with two other novels so as to pursue an argument about pattern and repetition in late modernist novels (pp. 459–66); James's realisation, looking at the lighthouse, that 'nothing was simply one thing' (*TtL*, p. 172) is cited by David Lodge as an image of the modernist novel itself (p. 495). These references define Woolf as a useful but marginal figure whose work is abstract, remote from realism, and interesting mainly as a way of describing the important phenomenon of modernism.

Serious critical endeavours other than the investigation of modernism have had rather little to say about Woolf. Wayne C. Booth's *The Rhetoric of Fiction* (1961), which did so much to begin discussion of narrative voices in fiction, pays little attention to her. It remarks only in a footnote on the vagueness of the term 'stream of consciousness' (p. 164), and dismisses *To the Lighthouse* as being only about sensibility (p. 143). Roger Fowler, and Geoffrey Leech and Michael Short, who have used tools from linguistics to describe the narrative voices of English fiction, have mentioned her only briefly (Fowler, 1986, p. 127; Leech and Short, 1981, *To the Lighthouse* mentioned on p. 340).

Marxist critics have not paid much attention to her either. When they have done so, they have quite rightly protested against ethereal readings; but while insisting on the importance of material and economic issues in fiction they have continued to see Woolf as avoiding them. In 1953 Arnold Kettle described *To the Lighthouse*, not as symbolic or as representing a 'stream of consciousness', but as being about things that are neither interesting nor important (pp. 91–9; 94). In 1970 Raymond Williams, who seldom discussed her novels, complained that *Mr Bennett and Mrs Brown* and 'Modern Fiction' argue in favour of fiction ignoring social and material circumstances in favour of the 'luminous halo' (Williams, 1970, p. 153). It has been left for feminist criticism to reveal the very close commitment in the novels to discussion of material experience.

This, then, is the background against which the ensuing discussion of much post-war criticism of *To the Lighthouse* is set. Virginia Woolf is regarded as a minor writer, who is at the same time historically significant as a modernist. Her novels are regarded as difficult and of puzzling forms, which are assumed to be intended to give a distanced portrayal of the workings of the human mind more accurately than a linear narrative; at the same time her work is thought of as remote from representations of real life, as poetic. Finally, the cult of the Bloomsbury group in the 1970s and 1980s has categorised her, and often her work, as class-bound and neurotic – a recent example of this being Hugh Kenner's *A Sinking Island* (1988) which, while describing England as a culture carelessly repudiating its own modernist glories, nevertheless consistently represents Virginia Woolf as faintly ridiculous.

A 'Structured' Text

New Criticism and its Followers: Symbolic and Allegorical Readings

In 1947 R. L. Chambers wrote that Virginia Woolf was not interested in what people do, only in what happened in their minds (Chambers, 1947, pp. 2–3). He cited business and India as things people do, not considering that these might also be experienced in the mind. The idea that Woolf's novels relate only to immaterial matters coincided with the idea of the followers of the New Criticism that all literary texts should be studied in terms of their internal structures and with no apparent reference to the material world. This resulted in a great many symbolic and allegorical interpretations, some of which are still being produced. Unfortunately this kind of criticism, although fun to write, is boring to read. It shuts out its readers' own experience of the text, imposing the critic's finished interpretation. Its suggestions often seem arbitrary.

What follows here is a detailed survey of this criticism of *To the Lighthouse*, which should be read, or skipped, simply as information.

In 1939 David Daiches described Woolf as one of an aristocratic tradition of writers who, faced with a complex and deteriorating society, succeed by retreating into the study to construct a refined system of thought or, as in her case, a series of personal observations (Daiches, 1939, pp. 158–65). He praised *To the Lighthouse* as her best book because its island setting allows it convincingly to avoid much reference to the rest of life (pp. 183–4). In 1945 he elaborated this reading by describing the events of the novel, and its rarefied setting, as being woven into a symbolically significant pattern (Daiches, 1945, pp. 77–92). Each character is seen as representing a precisely patterned function in relation to the others (pp. 78–84) and the lighthouse itself is taken as a symbol of the idea of the individual, at once unique and yet also part of the flux of experience (p. 84). Reaching the lighthouse is read as representing a character's arrival at a truth beyond him or herself, a reading that is extended to Lily as she finishes her painting when the others land (pp. 84–5). This symbolism is accompanied by another involving colours, in which red and brown, associated with Mr Ramsay until the end of the book, are colours of egotism, and blue and green, associated with Lily, are colours of impersonality. Mrs Ramsay's purple is placed between these extremes (pp. 85–6). A third symbol is seen emerging from repetitions and echoes within the book, whereby the thoughts of one character and the actions of another merge into a symbolic representation of the relation of individuals to the whole of existence (pp. 86–92).

Some critics see the novel as working both symbolically and realistically. Joan Bennett identifies both a 'prose plane' on which the reader is interested in human affairs (J. Bennett, 1964, p. 102), and another plane on which the lighthouse is a central symbol: its revolving stroke represents the alternation of joy and sorrow in human life and relationships, which alternation is itself also symbolised in the form of the book with its long and short parts and its tragic and optimistic events (pp. 103–5).

Michael Leaska also distinguishes between a 'prose level' (Leaska, 1977, pp. 147–50) and a 'stratum of poetry' (pp. 150–6), and, like Bennett, gives prominence to the latter by making it the climax of his discussion. His symbolic reading is elaborate. He sees the juxtaposition of the hedge and Mrs Ramsay as evolving into a symbol of an emotional blockage, finally resolved when Lily transfers her yearnings away from Mrs Ramsay and to Mr Ramsay in his distant boat (pp. 151–3). The lighthouse itself is a symbol of the ideal of human harmony, an ironic symbol at first when going to it is problematic, and also in 'Time Passes' when its beam appears indifferent to human affairs, but eventually representing achieved harmony (pp. 153–6).

Leaska's reading demonstrates how easily a symbolic exposition can be used to justify a particular interpretation. In arguing that harmony and emotional freedom, symbolised by the lighthouse, is possible only after Mrs Ramsay's death, Leaska is reinforcing a hostile account of Mrs Ramsay. He has been cited as the first critic to disapprove of her, although Pederson had already argued in 1958 that her children were prevented from reaching adulthood while she lived. Leaska disapproves because he views her entirely as a character who ought to be kind at all times to those in her house, and as one who fails to be kind, selfishly refusing Mr Ramsay's little request to be told she loves him at the end of 'The Window' (Leaska, 1977, p. 129). Mr Ramsay, however, is seen as more devoted to his family than she is, heroically honest, and self-pitying only as a result of his wife's coldness (p. 132). Her removal makes his, and Lily's, happiness possible. Leaska first mooted this argument in an earlier book (Leaska, 1970) in which he had tried, rather laboriously, to describe the novel as a series of contrasting narratives by each of the major characters.

As well as imposing interpretations on to the text themselves, symbolic readings also legitimise other readings which, without defining such specific detachable symbols, nevertheless see the novel as primarily offering abstract ideas encoded in the characters and plot.

N. C. Thakur acknowledged Daiches as an author who convinced him that Woolf's novels could really be understood only through their symbolism. He laboriously discusses the idea of symbolism, citing many authorities (Thakur, 1965, pp. 1 10), but when he comes to analyse the novels he actually does it only by sorting aspects of each novel into metaphoric clusters so as to explain his final interpretations. Thus he describes *To the Lighthouse* as contrasting men and women, men being associated with restlessness of intellect and with selfishness and egotism, with Mr Ramsay's striving up the alphabet and with the 'beak of brass', and women being associated, in both Mrs Ramsay and Lily, with intuition and mysticism and a desire for unity of experience (pp. 73–8). He sees the novel as representing the ideal of enlightenment overcoming strife, through this contrast and through allusions to religious ideas – he quotes William Bankes's vision of Mrs Ramsay as a Madonna and also Mr Ramsay's sharing of bread and cheese with the fishermen in the boat, which he sees as Christ-like (pp. 78–85).

The earliest example of a detailed reading which makes the whole novel into an allegory like this is Bernard Blackstone's. Blackstone defines Woolf as exploring moods and experiences which are transitory yet somehow eternal, being all part of an ultimate unity definable only through images (pp. 10–12). In his discussion of *To the Lighthouse* (pp. 99–130) he describes the house as the thing which binds the whole book together: in 'The Window' it warmly contains the opposing worlds of masculinity and femininity, in 'Time Passes' it has been deserted, in 'The Lighthouse' it is occupied only by the feminine, Lily trying to recreate Mrs Ramsay. In 'The Window' the house's warm enclosure is possible because of Mrs Ramsay, who is seen as bringing all life into the house and as making it timeless. After her removal from the novel we are, eventually, shown two contrasting movements, that of the young Ramsays into the future and that of Lily back into the past. This house, set on an island, is surrounded by the sea which represents a deeper reality than the one of doing and speaking, a reality into which humans eventually sink; but before they do so they are capable of comedy, which Blackstone sees especially in the doings of Mr Ramsay. A detailed description of the action and the characters of the novel is fitted into this perceived pattern so that it is described as having no plot, and no thesis, but as balancing so many aspects of life within a coherent form.

This is the kind of criticism most represented in Beja's *Casebook*. James Hafley's essay (Beja, 1970, pp. 133–48) argues, apparently arbitrarily, that the action of the novel is unimportant compared with its symbolic meaning. Aware that different critics already interpreted the lighthouse differently, he proposed that it be seen as part of a complex structure in which Mrs Ramsay, mainly important as a symbol, would be associated with the sea, and with ideas of continuity and fluidity, while Mr Ramsay would be associated with facts and with the land which is threatened by the sea. The novel thus becomes a confrontation between two kinds of truth, with Mr Ramsay's triumphing in 'Time Passes'; in 'The Lighthouse', however, Lily in her picture and Mr Ramsay in arriving at the lighthouse each achieve acceptance of the other's truth.

Norman Friedman (in Beja, 1970, pp. 149–68) criticises other critics for imposing single meanings on to the climax of the novel, the arrival at the lighthouse and the completion of Lily's picture; he answers them by working out an extremely complex scheme in which everything in the novel is linked with its own opposite, indicating a universal dialectic. At the end of the novel the surviving major characters accept the dialectic by moving from their own viewpoint to the opposite, and do so by committing themselves to transition, symbolised by the sea.

Sharon Kaehele and Howard German (in Beja, 1970, pp. 189–209) commented on the difference between different critics' interpretations, but insisted nevertheless that the novel has a single unified meaning based on the symbol of the lighthouse itself, which represents both Mr and Mrs Ramsay, seen as opposites, and their relationships with change. The voyage and Lily's effort to complete her picture are seen as processes in which the surviving characters learn to change existing prejudices and creatively accept new ones.

By the early 1960s this kind of reading was an orthodoxy, offered in simpler critical works. In 1963 A. D. Moody wrote that *To the Lighthouse* is solely about workings in the mind, which are indicated by the subtleties of the prose (Moody, 1963, pp. 30–1); and that the world of action, represented by Mr Ramsay (p. 31), is subordinated to the world of art and imagination, represented by Lily and by Mrs Ramsay who is herself in due course represented by the lighthouse (pp. 31–43). The world of art triumphs. In the same year Dorothy Brewster also saw Lily's achieved picture as the focal point of the novel, imposing meaning on the rest of it; many critics before and after her, including some recent feminist critics, have done the same.

Perhaps the most monumental study of this kind of *To the Lighthouse* is Alice van Buren Kelley's. Her book opens by quoting a passage from Woolf's diary in which 'fact' and 'vision' are contrasted, and proposes as its theme the pursuit of these terms through the novels (Kelley, 1973, pp. 1–6). Its long and detailed account of *To the Lighthouse* (pp. 114–43) is based on a reading of it as a study of the marriage of opposites, and of art as a way of learning to combine opposing ideas. Every detail of the novel, it seems, fits into this pattern. Mr and Mrs Ramsay are established, partly by references to the ideas of Hafley and Friedman, and of J. Graham who saw them as time and eternity, as polarities who are nevertheless harmoniously combined (pp. 115–16). 'The Window' is seen as the means by which the details of the polarity and the combination are established: Mr Ramsay is read in terms of the image of a blade; and as a devotee of abstract truth, who cannot perceive complete truth but who holds heroically and in isolation to the facts he has; and as, therefore, like the lighthouse (pp. 116–17). Mrs Ramsay is read as representing vision, creativity, and a difficult struggle to bring all aspects of life together, although Pederson's representation of her as a negative force is mentioned (pp. 118–19). She is associated with the sea, pulling between unity and formlessness, and the beam from the lighthouse that illuminates everything (pp. 119–20). The harmony between these two principles is represented by the Ramsays' marriage, which may include minor disputes but which is recognised by Lily as symbolising the whole of life (pp. 121–8). Lily struggles to represent this wholeness in art (pp. 128–9). 'Time Passes' is said to represent the ultimate defeat of disorder and the triumph of vision and of Mrs Ramsay, in her lighthouse beam and in the return of her family (pp. 131–4). In 'The Lighthouse', Kelley says, the lighthouse itself and the voyage to it must be read as symbols, though she cites various different interpretations, including those of Burra who saw it as perfection, Bennett, Kaehele and German, and C. B. Cox who interpreted the lighthouse as a symbol of the isolated individual and its beams as Mrs Ramsay's unifying love (pp. 135–7). Kelley makes the voyage signify both Mr Ramsay's recognition of the continuing importance and essence of his wife and her vision, and Cam's and James's discovery that the lighthouse is factual as well as imagined (pp. 137–9). Lily, meanwhile, is assisted in her completion of her picture, her vision of unity in life, when she calls on both Mr and Mrs Ramsay and Mrs Ramsay reappears before her as Mr Ramsay reaches the lighthouse (Kelley, 1973, pp. 139–43).

The persistent ingeniousness of this reading does not explain why, as is assumed, the novel must be read in this way, why its meaning has to be sought in metaphorical interpretation. This manner of reading is taken for granted. In a more recent (and simpler) book Kelley still proposes a very similar reading even after providing historical and biographical information putting the novel into a context beyond itself (Kelley, 1987).

Hermione Lee's Introduction clearly situates her book also as one that will discuss the novels in isolation, regarding Woolf's life and known views as irrelevant (Lee, 1977, p. 1). Its close reading of the text, however, does offer a rather more convincing explanation of why *To the Lighthouse* might be read allegorically. Dr Lee describes 'The Window' as a representational account of family life, in which the contrasting figures of Mr and Mrs Ramsay, and the action around them, are also made to suggest certain abstract qualities (pp. 117–30). This is partly because of the narrative technique which places particular details of a character's thought in the context of other aspects of the novel; partly because of the reiteration of details, such as the greenhouse roof or the banging of doors, which gradually take on textual significance; partly because of the image of the sea voyage, appearing in the fairy tale read to James as well as in the story itself; and also because of the creation of Mrs Ramsay as a figure endowed with mythical qualities by the narrator and by the other characters in the novel.

In 'Time Passes' the attempt by a watcher to find a meaning in life is thwarted by the chaos of events, though Mrs Ramsay becomes legendary in the mind of Mrs McNab (p. 130); but in 'The Lighthouse' Mr Ramsay accepts the reality of the lighthouse without melodrama, and Lily learns to make coherent shape with memories from which she achieves distance (pp. 130–6). The central preoccupation of the novel is therefore seen as the relationship between chaotic complexity and simple coherence, and the search for a balance between them. This is finally achieved by Lily, who both makes her picture and recreates Mrs

Ramsay, while Mr Ramsay simultaneously achieves heroic stature at the lighthouse. Dr Lee concludes (pp. 136–7) that the book has a distinct meaning, which is that art is a difficult but essential activity, the possibly painful act of working out truths about the relationship of life to death.

Another insistently symbolic reading of the novel also appeared in 1977 when Jack F. Stewart proposed that the lighthouse, through its light, stood for different aspects of spiritual vision, and in more recent years a number of critics have read the novel in a similar manner, sometimes more simplistically. Michael Rosenthal describes it largely in terms of its form which he sees as a balancing of details, and of the need for a unifying vision of all of life, which Cam and James and Lily all achieve only when they learn not to reject Mr Ramsay (Rosenthal, 1979, pp. 103–27). Velicu is concerned to discover what gives the novels form when Woolf has abandoned plot, which her essays tell him she has done, and reads *To the Lighthouse* as mirroring the novelist's activity in Lily's: both relate disparate material in a structured work of art. The structure of the novel, he argues, is provided by its references to the natural cycle, to images of completed actions, and to the sonnet form (Velicu, 1985, pp. 57–79). Apter also quotes 'Modern Fiction' and argues that *To the Lighthouse* is directly about the relationship between consciousness and an external world because it shows, repeatedly and in all its major characters, the process whereby events and even people become symbols within the mind of an onlooker (Apter, 1979, pp. 73–99). Meanwhile Martin Gliserman has argued in a lengthy article that the novel centres on the idea of the nurturing and creative female principle, and Bruce Bassoff, in another article, has argued that the whole novel focuses on the ideal of learning to accept alternative views of life. Even Janis Paul's investigation of social and historical references is subordinated to an argument in which Mrs Ramsay represents internal consciousness confronting the chaos of experience, and Lily's picture represents the realisation that these two aspects of life must both be accommodated (pp. 153–81).

Given this critical tradition, and in spite of the publication of Woolf's letters, including one to Roger Fry in which she wrote:

> I meant *nothing* by The Lighthouse. One has to have a central line down the middle of the book to hold the design together. . . . I can't manage Symbolism except in this vague, generalised way. . . . directly I'm told what a thing means, it becomes hateful to me. (27 May 1927; *Letters*, Volume 3, p. 385),

other readers have had to insist almost rebelliously on the existence of social and historical referents within the text. Lyndall Gordon's biography bravely reads 'Time Passes' specifically in terms of the First World War; so does Marianne Dekoven, and so did Hugh Stoddart and Colin Gregg in the making of their television film in 1983. Stoddart and Gregg also set their film in St Ives in Cornwall, where Woolf spent the summers in her own childhood and where Godrevy lighthouse itself echoes the novel far more convincingly than anywhere in the Hebrides, where the novel pretends to be set. These readings avoid the timidity of the text itself about its reference to time and place. But even feminist criticism has only recently turned from *A Room of One's Own* to realise that the novels also can be read as referring to experienced life, not just to variously imagined ultimate truths.

Mythological and Freudian Readings

Meanwhile, however, other critics have attempted to understand the novel in terms of archetypal myth. These readings are occasionally unconvincing, but are often more stimulating than the allegorical readings which work to close the text, and the reader, off from anything else.

Few, perhaps, have been at once so thorough and so arbitrary as F. L. Overcarsh, who read the novel as based on the Bible, seeing Mr and Mrs Ramsay as Adam and Eve because they walk in the garden (Overcarsh, 1950, p. 109), and Mrs Ramsay/Eve as falling from grace by taking the atheist Tansley for a walk and giving him her bag to carry after she has taken leave of Elsie, whose name is a derivative of both 'Alice', meaning 'truth', and 'Elizabeth', meaning 'consecrated to God' (pp. 109–10); later, Mrs Ramsay becomes Mary (p. 111) and the Roman Catholic Church (p. 112), and the soul of Christ returning to Lily (p.

117), and Mr Ramsay is the God of Wrath who becomes the God of Love taking everyone to the salvation of the lighthouse (pp. 118–19). Some later critics have referred to Overcarsh, but only as an extremist whom they do not follow.

Nevertheless two recent critics have seen the novel as a description of forms of religious, although not Christian, experience. Martin Corner argues that while Mrs Ramsay might easily be seen as representing an experience in which the self is fused with the rest of existence (Corner, 1981, p. 410), Lily's painting represents a mysticism in which the self confronts the world and perceives its wonder (pp. 413–16); and that Mr Ramsay achieves, as he stands before the lighthouse, a heroic selfless atheism which contrasts with Tansley's mean-spirited egoistic version (pp. 416–23). Mark Hussey, in contrast, reads all Woolf's fiction as an account of the human attempt to reconcile faith in creative individual existence with knowledge of human powerlessness, and of art as the place where the individual tries to defy powerlessness by asserting a meaning. In the course of this argument he sees Mrs Ramsay as representing a search for security through mystic union with nature (Hussey, 1986, pp. 31–2), and Lily's picture as any artist's struggle to assert a coherent vision with which to confront chaos (p. 73).

Several critics have turned instead to classical mythology, and to the readings of this mythology by Freud and Jung. This method of investigation of the possibilities of the text has generated far more ideas than the attempts at religious readings, and especially it has opened a debate about Mrs Ramsay which leads eventually into recent feminist debate.

In 1956 Joseph L. Blotner (Beja, 1970, pp. 169–88) dismissed Overcarsh's reading on the grounds that Woolf herself was certainly not a Christian and imposed instead a reading interpreting Mrs Ramsay as the ancient threefold Goddess appearing in legend as Rhea, the mother of Zeus, Demeter, goddess of the corn, and Persephone, the daughter of Zeus by Demeter, later stolen by Dis, the god of the underworld, and redeemed for half of each year by Demeter's sorrow and love. Blotner carefully insists that he is using this composite myth, and recent anthropological discussions of it as a universal archetype, as a way of reading, and is not attributing either deliberate or unconscious use of it to Virginia Woolf herself (Beja, 1970, pp. 169–72). His own use of it is heavy-handed, ignoring any possibility of irony within the novel, as when he asserts that Mr and Mrs Ramsay must be symbolic because Lily suddenly sees them as such while watching them watch their children playing (p. 172). His argument is that Mrs Ramsay, like Rhea, protects her children, especially the youngest who opposes him, from their father (pp. 173–4); that she is goddess-like with her beauty and her intuitive knowledge (pp. 174–5); that, like Demeter and unlike most of the Olympian deities, she is kind, accompanied by images of fruitfulness (pp. 175–6); that, like Demeter, who was celebrated by women in the Eleusinian mysteries, she represents female power (pp. 176–8); and that Mrs Ramsay's aspect of sorrow is like Demeter's sorrow for the loss of Persphone (p. 178). Mrs Ramsay then becomes Persephone, whose death or passage to the underworld is followed by the withdrawal of Demeter's gifts from the world and equated with the misery of 'Time Passes' (pp. 178–82), and whose annual return, like that of plants, is celebrated in the revival of the house, the new-found rapport between the Ramsays in the boat, and Lily's achieved painting (pp. 182–3). Finally, Blotner accompanies this reading of the novel as celebrating a female power with a brief discussion of the relationship between James and his parents as Oedipal: James is said to adore his mother, hate his father as a rival, and then move to a rapport with his father at the lighthouse (pp. 184–6). Blotner claims that these two myths reflect two fundamental aspects of human experience, the Oedipal one described by Freud and the Rhea/Demeter/Persephone one by Jung, and that the lighthouse itself, with its tower and its threefold stroke, represents both: and that the novel exalts the value of the female, which is loving and ameliorating. Females may die without loss to the world, because they have already nurtured new life (pp. 186–7).

This idea of female perfection as that which involves the self-sacrificial nurturing of others, and of Mrs Ramsay as some kind of image in relation to that ideal, is maintained in all criticism of *To the Lighthouse*, myth-criticism and other, until challenged by recent feminist criticism, in spite of the hurt this definition of perfection causes. Mitchell Leaska's criticism of Mrs Ramsay (see 'New Criticism and its Followers; Symbolic and Allegorical Readings' above) was based only on the assertion that she failed to nurture her menfolk properly; this demand is the only one against which he measured her.

In 1958 Glenn Pederson interpreted the novel as an account of James's Oedipus complex, but giving much more weight to this reading than Blotner, and blaming Mrs Ramsay for her son's difficulties. He sees her as short-sighted and unthinking, as dominating her family and friends by demanding their emotional allegiance (Pederson, 1958, pp. 585–7), as demanding James's alliance with her against his father (pp. 587–8), and as refusing union with her husband, even when they are alone together at the end of 'The Window' (pp. 588–91). She is even seen as symbolically preventing James from going to the lighthouse and to adulthood by agreeing the weather will be wet (p. 591). In 'The Lighthouse', after her death, James finally reaches the lighthouse and so identifies with his father (pp. 594–5); Cam is with them and capitulates willingly to the males, which she was unable to do before (pp. 592–4); and Lily achieves her picture when she perceives Mr Ramsay restored as the rightful head of the family (pp. 595–600).

This reading has been accepted, often only in part, by subsequent critics; ideas derived from it have been used even by recent feminist critics, who discuss the idea of the Oedipus complex rather differently, and who see Mrs Ramsay more positively.

Maria DiBattista argues that the novel originated in Woolf's own Oedipal struggle with the power of her writer father (DiBattista, 1980, pp. 64–9), but that it also offers an image of the mother as a source of life and vision (p. 69). The reading centres on James. His desired voyage to the lighthouse, to selfhood, is indeed achieved, after the prolonged night of 'Time Passes' (p. 70). The greatest threat to it was Mr Ramsay's aggressive insistence that only facts be thought about; and James finally confronts this aggression as he sits in the becalmed boat and, half-remembering what we know was the dispute between his parents in 'The

Window', imagines a wheel crushing a foot. DiBattista equates the Greek name Oedipus with the meaning 'swollen foot', and takes this near-memory as imaging James's psychic situation, in which he must destroy paternal tyranny in order to repossess the childhood paradise of his mother (pp. 70–3). His position is finally resolved as he not only steers the boat successfully and receives his father's praise, but also realises that the lighthouse is both the stark tower associated with his father and the distant eye associated with his mother's view of it. James takes on the complex ability, associated by DiBattista with the idea of androgyny, of thinking with both father and mother (pp. 105–10).

DiBattista also argues that all the marriages in the novel, real or projected, fail (pp. 77–94); and in 'Time Passes', as in the speech of Time at the beginning of Act IV of *The Winter's Tale*, everyone must wait for a new image of life to make itself known (pp. 94–100). This is achieved only when Lily again sees Mrs Ramsay on the step, and now manages to represent her by drawing a single line (DiBattista, 1980, p. 107).

Anne G. Hoffman again reads Mrs Ramsay as Demeter/Persephone, as an imaginary all-embracing mother (Hoffman, 1984, pp. 187–90). This is one of the few pieces of criticism to have made much use of Susan Dick's edition of the manuscripts of *To the Lighthouse* (1982). Hoffman argues that as she worked Woolf gradually refined Mr Carmichael into Mrs Ramsay's opposite, a Poseidon to her Demeter, a figure whose book is compared to a trident, who calms the waves and keeps civilisation going with his poetry and his lonely vigil through the night of 'Time Passes' (pp. 182–7). The novel becomes the story of Lily's involvement with Demeter, the source and protector of life, and her resistance to the marriage and sacrifice Demeter demands (p. 185); in 'Time Passes' Lily suffers separation from the mother figure (p. 193), and in 'The Lighthouse' she learns, under the guiding presence of the godlike poet, to acknowledge rather than suppress that loss and to put her experience into her picture, to find an articulation of her own life (pp. 194–5).

Hoffman's discussion is briefly related (p. 188) to some ideas of Nancy Chodorow, who has described female identity as more fluid than male identity because never fully separated from the fused mother–child relationship in babyhood. Hoffman does not go so far as to see the mothering Mrs Ramsay as a threat to Lily, a case argued earlier by Jane Lilienfeld. Lilienfeld saw Lily as confronting two aspects of archetypal femaleness in Mrs Ramsay: the archetypal mother whom Lily, like James and Mr Ramsay, longs to possess (Lilienfeld, 1977, pp. 349–58); and the destructive maternal power that involves the denial of self, the death of separate human identity, for mother and child, Demeter the mother of Persephone who accompanies her daughter into death as Mrs Ramsay accompanied Prue (pp. 358–66). Only after great suffering, Lilienfeld says, does Lily achieve acceptance of Mrs Ramsay as a person like herself, not as a dominating power, when Mrs Ramsay appears to return to her near the end of the book (Lilienfeld, 1977, p. 367). Lily is then able to turn her imagination to Mr Ramsay in his boat, a pitiable being (pp. 368–70), and to the other male characters, including the detached Augustus Carmichael, who alone resisted Mrs Ramsay's dangers (pp. 370–1). Lily learns as she finishes her painting, that she need not follow Mrs Ramsay but can be a self-sufficient woman doing her own independent work (p. 371).

These mythological and Freudian readings articulate more stimulating ideas about the meaning of the novel than the simpler allegorical readings. They do not, usually, claim to be explaining the one closed meaning of the text; instead they each offer a possibility, which the reader can explore along with other possibilities.

Readings in Aesthetic Theory

Another set of readings of this novel relates it to philosophical ideas discussed by members of the Bloomsbury group. These were first discursively described by J. K. Johnstone (1954), and have progressively taken on the status of a myth ever since then. Most critics writing about Woolf at any length make mention of the Cambridge philosopher G. E. Moore, who proclaimed the supreme value of certain states of consciousness involving human relationships and the enjoyment of beautiful objects, and who was adulated by the Cambridge friends of Virginia Woolf's brother, Thoby Stephen. But the discussion of him is invariably brief and merely ritualistic.

The original version of this kind of criticism, the early attempts to explain Woolf's work in terms of the ideas of Henri Bergson (see above), was dismissed by J. W. Graham (1956), although Jill Morris again referred to Bergson when arguing that *To the Lighthouse* indicates Woolf's lack of belief in objective truth (Morris, 1977, pp. 10 and 58–9).

Several critics, however, have turned to the ideas of Roger Fry in order to try to describe what they understand as Virginia Woolf's preoccupation with the nature of truth. Roger Fry was an artist and art historian, the organiser of the 1910 Post-Impressionist Exhibition that first brought the work of Cezanne and Van Gogh to London, and author of *Vision and Design* (1920), a collection of essays on aesthetic theory. He was also a friend whose biography Virginia Woolf wrote after his death in 1934.

In 1946 J. H. Roberts cited Fry's 'An Essay in Aesthetics' (*Vision and Design*, pp. 22–39) which insists on the self-containedness of works of art, and their lack of relevance to the world of action (Roberts, 1946, p. 835). Roberts, curiously, labels Woolf's Mrs Brown as her symbol for the same idea, a symbol decrying photographic representation, and then inevitably describes Woolf's novels as abandoning plot and representation in favour of what Picasso and Cezanne were doing in painting; according to Fry, these artists taught us that paintings achieve their effect solely through the relations of forms and colours, and not at all through anything they represent (Roberts, 1946, pp. 835–6). Roberts also quotes Fry as claiming that the contemplator of a work of art becomes absorbed in its forms to the extent that he experiences a real feeling of order, and that art therefore gives access to the order underlying the details of actual life; and he equates this idea with Woolf's supposed desire that the novel indicate an ultimate rather than a photographic truth (pp. 839–40). He then discusses *Mrs Dalloway* and *To the Lighthouse* as examples of attempts to build fiction on the conviction that only form is significant in works of art. He argues that *To the Lighthouse* discusses the relationships between both humans and forms, and indicates that the one between forms is more permanently significant. Mrs Ramsay, he writes, attempts to create beauty among people but fails, although when she shrinks to a 'wedge-shaped core of darkness' (*TtL*, p. 60), and when her dinner party composes itself into shape when the candles are lit, she is recognising the significance of form. Lily, the artist, however, actually creates order by using shape and colour (Roberts, 1946, pp. 844–6).

Keith M. May describes Lily as the equivalent of the novelist herself, and as an artist striving for significant form according to the doctrines not only of Fry but also of Woolf's brother-in-law Clive Bell in his book *Art* (1914) (May, 1967, pp. 91–2). Lily is said to confront the three problems of colours, light and shade, and the relations of masses, and to represent in these problems the major features of the whole novel. Colours are equated with the flux of perceptions and with femininity, relations of masses with the form of the novel and with masculinity, and light and shade with the alternation of the strokes of the lighthouse, and of the three sections of the novel (pp. 92–4). The conclusion is that in resolving these three problems and completing her picture Lily represents the author's success in finding a rigid design that gave form to her multiple memories and thoughts (May, 1967, p. 98).

However, Ruby Cohn had argued that while the novel initially opposes life and Mrs Ramsay to art and Lily (Cohn, 1962, pp. 128–9), nevertheless art is shown to depend upon the life it imitates: Lily's art derives from the life she observes; and although Mrs Ramsay is absent from Lily's second picture – the single line replacing the purple triangle – just as she is absent from the lighthouse when the other Ramsays reach it, nevertheless that painting, like that voyage, is dependent on her (pp. 130–1).

These suggestions are all ingenious, but they are repressive, each fitting the novel into one closed meaning. They are also confusing because they try to equate theories about non-representational form in art with the words in the novel, which claim to be representational.

Potentially more helpfully, Allen McLaurin proposed that Fry and Woolf should be compared in terms of their problems rather than their opinions, and particularly their anxieties about representation in art (McLaurin, 1973, p. 17). Fry is described, not as a fixed theorist, but as evolving and debating his ideas, moving away from and back towards allowing both formalism and representation in his account of art (McLaurin, 1973, pp. 18–25). His influence on Woolf is put beside that of Samuel Butler, who argued that life is irrational, and regarded form and convention in art as more important than moral argument (McLaurin, 1973, pp. 4–6). Woolf is described as questioning attempts at realistic representation in her progress from novel to novel, and *To the Lighthouse* is discussed at the end of McLaurin's book as a crystallisation of her debate. In this detailed discussion of the novel, however, McLaurin simply imposes on it yet another set of closing and defining descriptions, listing a number of ways in which it supposedly imitates a painting (pp. 177–206).

In exciting contrast, however, Thomas G. Matro proposed a reading that would acknowledge Fry's ideas as important, but would see the novel as opening a debate with them, rather than as formed by them. Matro argues that the tradition of trying to impose Fry's ideas on it has obscured a crucial irony in the novel: its demonstration that human relations and aesthetic relations are actually both unsatisfactory, even though its characters search for fulfilment in both (Matro, 1984a, pp. 212–13).

He says that Lily, far from achieving a perception of ultimate unity at the end of the novel, as so many critics assume, actually has to learn that such a thing is impossible. In 'The Window', when she is trying both to paint her picture and to understand Mrs Ramsay, she talks confidently about her aesthetic ideals, especially to William Bankes, and these ideals resemble Fry's ideas about the supremacy of unifying design; at the same time she also wants unity or 'oneness' with Mrs Ramsay (Matro, 1984a, pp. 213–14). But Lily's own way of thinking repeatedly shows not unity but ambivalence and frequent switches from one opinion to its opposite, as for example in her opinions of both William Bankes and Mr Ramsay (Matro, 1984a, pp. 214–15).

Matro argues that this pattern of alternatives and contradictions, of 'yes . . . but', actually dominates the whole novel from its opening, and is in direct contrast to Lily's ideals, and also to those of Mrs Ramsay herself, whose dinner party actually unifies only for one moment between separations; and that while most critics have described Lily's painting and Mrs Ramsay's dinner party as creating shape and unity, they actually, on the contrary, represent not unity but the process of wanting it and finding it impossible (pp. 215–19).

In 'The Lighthouse' Lily at first still equates the ideas of unified truth through art and of the permanence she thinks Mrs Ramsay could achieve ('Life stand still . . . ', *TtL*, p. 151). But then, thinking of her picture put away in an attic, she rejects the commonplace that art is permanent; and gradually she also realises that her picture should capture not a 'vision' but 'that very jar on the nerves' (*TtL*, p. 178), not a 'truth' but the act of thinking (Matro, 1984a, p. 219). Similarly she also discovers that learning to know people is not a matter of achieving union with them but of making up stories about them (*TtL*, p. 161); and the end of the novel is not triumphant (Matro, 1984a, p. 220). And James's experience mirrors Lily's in that he also learns to abandon his childhood vision and to accept the existence not of truth but of the process of thinking, as he distances old images about his father (Matro, 1984a, pp. 221–2).

This reading begins to challenge much of the existing criticism of the novel, not only that which relates it to Fry. It challenges the assumption that the novel represents an object, an idea, which is static and can, once discovered, be defined by a detached and objective reader; it does this by suggesting instead that the novel proposes that assumption through Lily and then undermines it, so that the reader is always faced with a process, a puzzle, rather than a statement.

This is quite a radical challenge: it begins to describe the reading as a process, not as a conclusion reached after the novel is finished. It was greeted with dismay later in the same year and in the same journal, when Daniel J. Schneider (1984) tried to insist that the point of Lily is her search for unity through art, and Matro replied that that was precisely what he disputed.

David Dowling, who again asserts Woolf's interest in Fry's ideas (Dowling, 1985, pp. 96–8), uses these to lead his discussion of *To the Lighthouse* only to a conventional description of the novel itself as an achieved aesthetic design encompassing and unifying diverse states of mind (pp. 148–62). Patrick J. Whiteley argues again that Woolf's essays show she wanted fiction to embody a more transcendent truth than that of everyday details, an idea partly derived from Fry (Whiteley, 1987, pp. 147–51); and that *To the Lighthouse* carefully separates subjective and objective perception and then demonstrates a true perception when these are synthesised by Lily and James at the end (pp. 183–95).

Whiteley's discussion is entitled 'Subject, Object, and the Nature of Reality: *To the Lighthouse*'. He is only the latest critic to refer to Andrew's description of his father's work (*TtL*, p. 26) as somehow summarising the whole novel; but this, just as when it was used thirty years earlier by Friedman (in Beja, 1970, p. 150), is only another restricting device for closing off the anxiety of reading this very open text.

The Narrative Voice

The kinds of criticism I have described so far are epitomised in a book by Avrom Fleishman (*Virginia Woolf, A Critical Reading*, 1975). In its chapter on *To the Lighthouse* (pp. 96–134) it incorporates all the established approaches. But it avoids discussing the most immediate feature of *To the Lighthouse* to new readers: its narrative voice.

None of the ideas that I have described really engages with the problem indicated by the earliest reviews, the unfamiliarity of the actual experience of reading *To the Lighthouse*, and indeed most of Woolf's fiction. It all leads away from that experience into interpretations that are thought out after the process of reading has been completed, and are then imposed retrospectively on the text.

Some recent critics, however, have engaged more directly with the form of the narration. Some of these have continued to make of this an exercise in which the thing ultimately under discussion is a meaning derived from the whole text after reading is complete. McLaughlin, for example, argued that the narrative voice knows all about the characters while they themselves have only very partial knowledge, and that the narrative voice is therefore Woolf's own wish-fulfilment (McLaughlin, 1981, pp. 185–6). Howard Harper proposed the evolution of the narrative consciousness through Woolf's novels as the theme of his book (Harper, 1982, pp. 1–2), but he actually merely describes the stories of the novels as stories of the characters' changes in consciousness. L. P. Ruotolo appeared to offer an examination of interruptions in Woolf's work, out of which come inventive energies (Ruotolo, 1986, p. 1); but these interruptions turn out not to be textual interruptions or disjunctions, but moments within the described events of each novel. He does see the final events of *To the Lighthouse* as inconclusive, even irrelevant, and interestingly relates this inconclusiveness to the idea of modernism as a process of openness and change within a text (p. 141). Ruotolo contrasts this with Mrs Ramsay's organising activities, which he sees as representing a Victorian assertion of wholeness (p. 123). But this modernism and Victorianism are discussed as ideas, not experiences in the reading. Ruotolo's methods are similar to those of John Burt (1982), who argued that both *To the Lighthouse* and *A Room of One's Own* apparently argue for new, modern, changes in society and thought while presenting idealised and nostalgic pictures of pre-war life. Both claim that the texts hold these opposing ideas in tension with each other, but they do not directly suggest how they might affect the reading experience.

Earlier, in 1973, James Naremore did directly discuss the narrative techniques of the novel. He wrote in his Introduction that reading Virginia Woolf is like being immersed so deeply in moving liquid that one can gain only muffled impressions of people and things (Naremore, 1973, p. 2), and gave a detailed account of *To the Lighthouse*, describing how this effect is created (pp. 112–50). He discusses the single narrative voice (pp. 113–18), and the way it supposedly conveys the characters' unarticulated feelings while obscuring the details of setting and dialogue (pp. 126–32); and the lack of interest in the characters' physical appearances (pp. 119–20); and the distancing effects of

'Virginia Woolf's' own stylisations (pp. 133–4). But in all this account he assumes that the narrative voice we hear is directly the voice of Virginia Woolf; and that she chooses to report her characters obscurely, although they exist somewhere else clearly enough.

He writes that it is difficult to define the relationship of author to characters, and goes on to examine some passages that are, he says, clearly authorial comment, and others that might be that, or might be examples of a character's stream of consciousness (pp. 120–6). He comments that in passages of apparently omniscient narration Woolf's voice lacks the confidence of, for example, George Eliot, giving way often to the thoughts of the characters (p. 126).

So the effect of this discussion is not in the end very stimulating to an attempt to articulate the reading experience itself, both because it is presenting a set of reflections reached long after the reading is over, and also because it represents the text so firmly as Virginia Woolf's obscure description of things that exist and that she alone has knowledge of.

A reader's attempt to define his or her experience of the novel may be undermined by any account describing what 'Virginia Woolf' is doing, whether it is constructing symbols, or putting together a 'poetic' whole, or describing pre-existing things in an idiosyncratic way. 'Virginia Woolf' is assumed to be authoritative. But discussions which separate the idea of the author from the idea of the narrative voice, the voice we interact with as we read, allow us to watch ourselves reading, and to try out articulations of that experience.

Two critics seem to me to help very much in this way, and to do so partly by means of linguistic criticism, criticism that uses ideas relating to the study of language itself. One is John Mepham in his 'Figures of Desire: Narration and Fiction in *To the Lighthouse*' (1976). The other is J. Hillis Miller in his 'Mr Carmichael and Lily Briscoe: The Rhythm of Creativity in *To the Lighthouse*' (1983).

Mepham distinguishes clearly between the 'fiction', which is all the things that are imagined to happen, and the narration, which indicates, explicitly or not, the causal relationships existing between them (p. 151); and he makes several general points about the narration.

The order in which the narration proceeds may not be the same as the imagined order of events: Mepham contrasts the opening of the narration, Mrs Ramsay's reply to James's unheard question, with the chronological order of the events within the novel, some early events only being described later, through various forms of flashback (p. 151).

The narration can make connections between events which are not connected in the fiction, for example by putting two events side by side so that they stand in a metaphorical relation to each other (p. 151).

The narration also makes the *telos* of the novel, the endpoint to which all parts of the narration relate. In a traditional novel, says Mepham – in the novels of Bennett, for example, though Mepham does not name him – the *telos* of narration and fiction might be the same, as the novel might describe a chronological sequence of events which are seen all to lead up to one concluding final event. But a different kind of novel will offer a different kind of relationship between events, and the narrative's *telos* will differ from the chronological order within the fiction (p. 152). *To the Lighthouse* is such a novel, one in which the point, or significance, of the events described is not a final state of affairs reached at the end.

Most of Mepham's article describes the workings of the narration of *To the Lighthouse*. From his account, which really should be studied in full, I derive two particular insights.

The first is that there is a direct contrast between 'The Window' and 'The Lighthouse' in the way the sequence of the narrative is managed (Mepham, 1976, p. 155). In 'The Window' there are two short sections (2 and 15) which re-establish continuity after the narrative has moved away from the chronology of events; section 2 (*TtL*, p. 19) returns us to the conversation about the trip to the lighthouse, and section 15, which is two lines long (*TtL*, p. 75), is Prue's reply to her mother's question, asked at the end of section 13 (*TtL*, p. 70), about whether Nancy went with Paul and Minta and Andrew on the walk from which they have not yet returned. Also, section 14 (*TtL*, pp. 70–4) is bracketed in round brackets and inserts a flashback; the round brackets indicate that this flashback is a digression within the narration, not a sudden jump within the fiction itself, and that the chronological sequence of events within the fiction is undisturbed. So in 'The Window' the narrative maintains a series of metonymic transitions from one event to the next: one thing is described and then the narrative describes another which is in some way clearly contiguous to the first within a single line of thought. Moreover that single line of thought is clearly marked and is brought back when necessary to the chronological process of events within the fiction.

In 'The Lighthouse', however, a different process is at work. Here there are two short sections in *square* brackets – section 6 (*TtL*, p. 167) and section 9 (*TtL*, p. 174) – which describe events happening at the same time as the things described in the main narration but not otherwise connected. (Although Mepham does not say so, the same is true of the square-bracketed insertions in 'Time Passes'.) The relationship between these sections and the longer ones surrounding them is a metaphoric one: the brief narration of one event suddenly substitutes for the longer narration of another, which it interrupts, and with which it connects figuratively. Mepham explains this later in the article, in a detailed discussion of these two moments in the text (pp. 181–4).

This suggestion that the progression of the narration in 'The Window' is predominantly metonymic, but that it is metaphoric in 'The Lighthouse', with its two stories held in a relationship of potential and actual substitution of one for the other, revolutionised my own experience of the novel when I first came on it. For the first time I found myself able to articulate my experience in reading: in 'The Window' I lead on with the narrator from one idea to the next, which is contiguous to, suggested by, its predecessor. In 'The Lighthouse' I substitute one scene for another, linking them in spite of their differences and also contrasting them. The question that must arise now concerns 'Time Passes'; but we will come to that later.

The second insight I derive from Mepham concerns the characteristics of the novel's narrative voice. Like Auerbach he asks who speaks in *To the Lighthouse* (p. 156). He replies by analysing the novel's use of what other critics have called free indirect discourse, and which he calls indirect attribution (p. 156). This is when a character's thoughts are narrated, not in direct speech indicated by quotation marks, but in reported thoughts which are not unambiguously presented as having their source only in the mind of the character described: they are infiltrated by the narration itself. This is the phenomenon often referred to as 'stream of consciousness', but Mepham's point is that such passages not only describe the thoughts, or consciousness, of the character, but also involve the consciousness of a narrative voice. He explains this by commenting on the suppression of referents that would attribute statements clearly to one source. In this passage, for example,

> their heads were pressed down by some remorseless gale. Speak to him they could not. They must come; they must follow. (*TtL*, p. 185)

the suppression of an attribution indicating whose thoughts these are means that the statement might relate not to Cam's and James's thoughts but to the narrator's (Mepham, 1976, p. 157).

And Mepham's main point is that the position and identity of that narrator remain elusive; there is no answer to the question about who speaks, except that somebody does. He argues that this indeterminacy in the attribution of thoughts is used throughout the novel so as to construct the narrative, as opposed to the fictional, order: to allow the *telos* to operate so that different events are connected and made meaningful in relation to each other (pp. 162–9). He gives a major example of this by indicating the recurrence of particular words and phonemic patterns in different parts of the novel, which links together the different stages of James's Oedipal struggle.

J. Hillis Miller's (1983) essay enters its discussion from a different viewpoint, a discussion of the nature of human creativity. In 'Virginia's Web' (1961) Geoffrey Hartman had suggested that art is the attempt, and the ability, to project the imagination so as to fill the gap, the void, that can threaten in anything; he also argued that any work of art undercuts itself by trying to assert that the void does not exist, that the world as we see it is real (Hartman, 1961, pp. 42–3). He read *To the Lighthouse* as confronting us with this tension, in the opposition between Mr and Mrs Ramsay's ways of thinking (Hartman, 1961, pp. 50–1). Hillis Miller took this up, although in an essay on Woolf's last novel, *Between the Acts*, he had suggested that creativity was not a matter of filling perceived gaps but of projecting the imagination forwards, following a sequence of thinking as far as possible (Miller, 1983, pp. 212–16). Into his demonstration of this idealist argument he introduces evidence derived both from *To the Lighthouse*'s contents, or fiction, and from careful linguistic inspection of the text.

He distinguishes four forms of creativity within the fiction: Mrs Ramsay's domestic creativity which ends, however, with death and with the war; Mr Ramsay's desire, and failure, to reach Z, and success in reaching the lighthouse with James and Cam; Lily's picture, completed at the same moment; and Augustus Carmichael's poetry (Miller, 1983, pp. 169–71).

The novel itself, Miller argues, represents a successful act of creativity: its imagined events have been projected forwards and are now narrated from the point of their completion; the narrative voice recreates them, retrospectively, and presents them to the reader for him or her, in turn, to recreate also (Miller, 1983, p. 172).

Miller, like Auerbach and Mepham, asks who the narrator is (p. 172). He replies in terms of the narrator's ability to speak for all the characters, from within their minds, in indirect discourse, in third-person past-tense constructions. He comments that the narrator, placed at an indeterminate time after the completion of the action and looking back, has no personal characteristics of his or her own, but moves without warning from mind to mind; but that this narrator is sometimes subversive, sometimes ironic, distancing itself from the character by suddenly interpolating 'he thought' or 'she thought' (pp. 172–4). He also says that it knows only what the characters know but, because it is reliving their lives, not living them for the first time, it sees everything they know from the vantage point of their future, their ending; and he describes the pathos of this extreme and disquieting example of the Victorian convention of the omniscient narrator, in which people are presented only as ghosts in the past (p. 174).

He goes on to suggest, ingeniously if fancifully, that this narrative presence might be embodied in Augustus Carmichael; that because Carmichael's detached mind is hidden from us his manner and the narrator's are similar (pp. 177–8).

Miller then turns to 'Time Passes', where the narrator's mind does, after all, operate without operating through the workings of the characters' minds. Here there are no human witnesses to events. We are presented with an attempt, indeed, to think of the kitchen table when one is not there, even though thinking of something depends on one's being there to think it. The only consciousness there before the preparations for the family's return begin, apart from Mrs McNab in her sporadic appearances, is that of the narrator, now a godlike all-seeing impersonal narrator who sees the disintegration that follows from the withdrawal of human consciousness. When humans are gone, 'Time Passes' seems to indicate, there will still be a witness, an inhuman one, of the desolation (Miller, 1983, pp. 178–81).

But there is something even more desolate to come. The remaining voice is not, says Miller, after all so impersonal, so unhuman. On the contrary, 'Time Passes' is full of personifications – of the airs, the lighthouse beam, the plants in the garden. 'Time Passes', Miller says, draws attention to the habit of personification, and so to the way in which ordinary language itself always personifies, always makes one think of objects – winds, houses, 'Mr Ramsay', 'Lily' – as if they were people.

One cannot think of anything, a table for example, without language. Language exists before the thought. And language creates in the thought the belief in the existence of selves. We can think only by means of such fictions (pp. 181–3).

The novel itself is the highly organised form of the unavoidable potentiality of language to create our way of understanding, which is ultimately – if 'ultimately' is a possible concept – only an illusion, a fiction. It shows how we think in terms of identities, believe in those identities, but how those identities are only created by the language in which we think (Miller, 1983, p. 182).

Finally Miller turns to one more question about the narrative voice: whether it is gendered. To this we shall return.

A 'Feminist' Text

Virginia Woolf and Feminism

A feminist critic begins by taking notice whenever it is assumed that all normal people are male. This assumption may be present in the text she or he reads and also in the act of reading.

Feminist literary criticism of the 1970s and 1980s has offered various ways of trying to demonstrate the prevalence of the assumption in members of both sexes, and of beginning both to explain and to correct it. It has taken Virginia Woolf's *A Room of One's Own* as a crucial description of its enterprise; and Virginia Woolf herself has been adopted as an honorary and distinguished member of the feminist movement. The discussion of her novels, and perhaps especially of *To the Lighthouse*, by feminist critics has often been influenced by their interest in her life and in *A Room of One's Own*.

A Room of One's Own is an attractively nostalgic text. It posits the pre-First World War world as a time when the sexes were more equal, as John Burt (1982) has demonstrated. It also offers safely romantic images of the exclusion of women from the world of scholarship and writing, so that readers can indulge dreams of the sad story of Judith Shakespeare, or of being excluded from the lawns of a Cambridge college, and can feel justly angry in terms of those dreams. But the dreams allow the dreamer to forget the real difficulties of excluded groups now – of really poor women, of Blacks. They perpetuate a very English ideal of timeless privilege that should be available to all, and they avoid interrogating the idea of privilege itself. Perhaps that is why *A Room of One's Own* is so popular.

As well as these images of social exclusion, it also offers images of ways in which women are prevented from articulating their own experience, which is assumed to be necessarily different from that of men. The second half of *A Room of One's Own* is based entirely on the idea that women have wanted to write but have been unable to do so because the language in which they might be able to articulate their experience does not exist. This idea has become a major part of much contemporary feminist critical theory, but it contains a certain confusion within itself.

In Chapter 4 *A Room of One's Own* surveys the history of women's writing in England from the late sixteenth century, very much as the novel *Orlando* does. And as in *Orlando* although less dramatically, we are presented with the imagined figure of a woman who wishes to be a writer but who is faced, as she confronts successive generations, with discouragements of successive kinds, until at last, at the end of the eighteenth century, things become easier for her: 'The middle-class woman began to write' we are told (*AROOO*, p. 63). As the narrative enters the nineteenth century it becomes even clearer that the image is that of a personality who exists prior to the act of writing. In her manifestation as Jane Austen she is praised for having written novels which show no sign of the circumstances of their author, of the social pressures against her writing at all; but in her manifestation as Charlotte Brontë she is found to have allowed her own passion to intrude and disrupt *Jane Eyre* (pp. 63–6). Clearly the assumption is that the author exists as a fully formed personality, containing her genius within her, before she writes, and also that the ideal novel exists somewhere too, as something she will manage to realise only if the relationship between herself and her novel is unproblematic.

> the woman who wrote those pages had more genius in her than Jane Austen; but if one reads them over and marks that jerk in them, that indignation, one sees that she will never get her genius expressed whole and entire. (*AROOO*, pp. 66–7)

Jane Austen apart, women writers have not yet, *A Room of One's Own* goes on to argue, reached that unproblematic relationship. As it moves on from Charlotte Brontë into the later nineteenth century, Chapter 4 describes the continuing difficulty, in one of its most quoted passages, as the absence of a tradition of women's writing, of literary mothers to think back through, and the absence in novels by men of a woman's sentence that the would-be woman writer might try to use for a model (pp. 72–5).

Chapter 5 demonstrates the continuing absence of a woman's sentence, and of literary models or traditions by means of which a woman might write her experience. Then in the sixth and final chapter the narrator allows herself the image of a woman and a man getting together into a taxi and driving off as people of equal significance (p. 92), and a dream of androgyny, of a universal ability to entertain both masculinity and feminity within the mind, to be achieved when women's writing will have as much of a tradition to draw on as men's (pp. 92–100). In the final 'peroration' (pp. 106–8) the female audience of the lecture *A Room of One's Own* purports to be is instructed to work extremely hard so as to create the tradition their descendants will be able to use.

This idea of androgyny is much disputed, but it is quite clear that it is a concept in which masculinity and femininity are both held to exist. It is not an image of the abolition of sexual difference, of women becoming like men. The point of it is that it allows the narrator to imagine a state of affairs when normal people will no longer be assumed to be male, and when that which is thought of as specifically female will be respectable, important, not 'required to be held back' (*AROOO*, p. 93). It is an image of the state of affairs which feminist critics still want to achieve.

But there are problems, which remain unresolved. One follows from the idea that men and women are all capable of both masculine and feminine thinking: this tends to perpetuate familiar stereotypes of what masculine and feminine are, and so to perpetuate the role models available to people defining themselves as female.

Another is the confusion at the heart of the argument that women have wanted to write, to describe their own lives, but that the appropriate language does not exist. On the one hand this seems to imply that, just like *A Room of*

One's Own's composite woman writer, these women and their experience exist somewhere fully formed before their language is invented; but on the other hand it implies that without the language articulation is impossible, and therefore implies that the women writers, and their defined experience, cannot have existed if the language defining them did not exist.

Feminist criticism tries to occupy both these positions. Some critics are involved in recovering the work of women who did indeed write but whose work has been, for various reasons, excluded from attention. Their assumption, broadly, is that women writers write differently from men, and they are engaged in defining the female tradition, which also involves re-reading those women writers who, like Virginia Woolf, have achieved canonical status. Others work within post-structuralist ideas which assert that language precedes and forms perception, and that experience cannot be thought of as existing in defined forms ready to be described. They read texts in terms of ideas, derived largely from the work of French theorists, about the relationship of language itself to gender distinction, and they associate these ideas with Woolf's idea of women as lacking the power of language.

Both kinds of criticism have addressed themselves to *To the Lighthouse*. But they merge rather than diverge. This is partly, though not wholly, because of the established habit of thinking of the novel as autobiographical.

Biographical Readings

The enterprise of recovering or re-reading the work of women writers of the past has often included an interest in the lives of those women. This is especially true in the case of Virginia Woolf, and has directly affected readings of *To the Lighthouse*, which has been seen as autobiographical ever since the early critics.

In recent years there has been a vigorous and at times acrimonious debate about Virginia Woolf's life. A definitive biography by her nephew Quentin Bell appeared in two volumes in 1972, following the five volumes of autobiography by her husband Leonard Woolf. In both Quentin Bell's and Leonard Woolf's work Virginia is described as prone to recurrent periods of madness. The meaning of the word 'mad' is not queried. The symptoms of her madness are described, but its cause is not much considered: the assumption is that it was physical, probably hereditary, and that it led eventually to her suicide at the age of 59 in 1941. Attacks followed the death of her mother in 1895 and of her father in 1904. Her marriage to Leonard in 1912 was followed by a lengthy period of madness, from which she did not recover until 1915. Leonard decided, with advice from certain doctors, that they should not have children, and spent the rest of their married life nursing and guiding Virginia so that attacks did not, until the end, overwhelm her.

More material has followed, especially her *Letters* and her *Diaries*, and also *Moments of Being*, a collection of previously unpublished autobiographical writings which contain reminiscences of her childhood and youth. A selection from her diaries was published earlier by Leonard in *A Writer's Diary*.

To all this material other writers have brought particular interests in the nature of madness, especially madness in women, and also the idea that, as a woman writer, Virginia Woolf may have been faced, like her woman writer in *A Room of One's Own*, with a society, a culture, in which it was impossible for her to articulate her own experience.

Other biographies have followed. Roger Poole's *The Unknown Virginia Woolf* (1978) argued that her madness was entirely the product of her circumstances: that she was, as the essays in *Moments of Being* indicate, sexually molested by her half-brothers in childhood and in young adulthood; that she was dominated by her demanding father after her mother's death when she was 13; and that Leonard, with his extreme insistence on rational argument and his lack of understanding of her sexual anxiety re-enacted that domination all through their marriage. Leonard, it is suggested, chose the doctors who would forbid children, thus depriving Virginia of her female identity; again, chose doctors who recommended seclusion, idleness, and much eating during Virginia's illnesses, and these treatments actually exacerbated her distress; and failed to understand her books although he praised them to her. Stephen Trombley's *'All That Summer She Was Mad': Virginia Woolf and Her Doctors* (1981) proposes comparable ideas, emphasising especially the inappropriateness of her medical treatment.

Phyllis Rose's *Woman of Letters, A Life of Virginia Woolf* (1978) is much less extreme but argues a specifically feminist case. Rose sees Virginia's life as tormented by her childhood, in which her mother devoted herself too much to the satisfaction of her husband's every whim so that after her mother's death Virginia was confronted by insatiable masculine demands. It argues that Leonard never understood what help she needed to overcome the results of this, and it gives great prominence to Virginia Woolf's passion for another woman, Vita Sackville-West. It sees Virginia Woolf as needing and seeking a specifically female context in her life.

More recently Lyndall Gordon's *Virginia Woolf, A Writer's Life* (1984) represented her not only as a woman who indeed had some innate liability to mental illness, the details of which cannot now be definitely established, but also as a woman whose difficulties were increased by her gender and by the assumptions about women that predominated in her circle. Other writers, such as Jean O. Love in *Virginia Woolf: Sources of Madness and Art* (1977), many of those in *Recollections of Virginia Woolf* edited by Joan Russell Noble (1972), and Richard Kennedy in *A Boy at the Hogarth Press* (1972) and John Lehmann in *Virginia Woolf* (1975), conform generally to Bell's idea of a frail invalid who was also a genius.

In contrast, another American scholar, Jane Marcus, has constructed another reading of Virginia Woolf's life and writings. During the 1980s Professor Marcus has edited three volumes of essays, and produced two collections of her own essays, all about Virginia Woolf. In the first of these books she included an essay, 'Thinking Back Through Our Mothers' (Marcus, 1981, pp. 1–30; reprinted Marcus, 1988, pp. 73–100), in which she claims Virginia Woolf as a revolutionary writer who confronted the system of patriarchy and the dominance of men in all her writing, and who suffered, not madness, but terror at the danger of doing so. In two subsequent essays, '"Taking the Bull by the Udders": Sexual Difference in Virginia Woolf – a Conspiracy Theory' (Marcus, 1987a, pp. 146–69, revised Marcus, 1987b, pp. 136–62) and 'Sapphistry: Narration as Lesbian Seduction in *A Room of One's Own*' (Marcus, 1987b, pp. 163–87), she reads *A Room of One's Own*, especially, as a covert lesbian attack on the male worlds of the university and of publishing. These essays argue that *A Room of One's Own* is written in a kind of code, and that its proper meaning would be picked up by a chosen audience of women with feminist and even lesbian sympathies, but missed by others, especially the men. The essays proceed by elucidating references to books and people within Woolf's text, such as *A Room of One's Own*'s reference to 'J – H – herself' (*AROOO*, p. 18), who is Jane Harrison the Cambridge anthropologist and student of Greek mythology, recently dead in 1929, and, Professor Marcus suggests, possibly the lover of another woman (Marcus, 1987b, p. 180); and to Oscar Browning, the leader of a group of homosexual misogynists within King's College; and by ranging such references into a system allegedly telling the listeners to the lecture to choose a female mentor rather than one among the men at King's (Marcus, 1987b, p. 181). She also relates *A Room of One's Own* to the trial of Radclyffe Hall's lesbian novel *The Well of Loneliness* for obscenity, ongoing in 1928 (Marcus, 1987b, p. 161), and elucidates the moment when the lecturer asks for assurance that 'Sir Charles Biron' is not eavesdropping as she talks of Chloe liking Olivia (*AROOO*, p. 78) by telling us that the presiding magistrate at the trial was Sir Chartres Biron (Marcus, 1987b, p. 166). These references are put together to construct an alternative meaning to the text, so that *A Room of One's Own* becomes an essay in code, a protest against the outlawing of lesbianism, and Virginia Woolf becomes a deliberate advocate of lesbianism. In her most recent volume, *Art and Anger* (1988), Jane Marcus collects a trio of her essays in which she has openly confronted and denounced Quentin Bell's version of his aunt's life, and his insistence that she was not a feminist (Marcus, 1988, pp. 157–212). Professor Marcus has certainly claimed the legendary character of Virginia Woolf for radical feminism. Other Americans, including Joanne Trautmann, one of the editors of the *Letters*, in her Introduction to a volume of essays celebrating the centenary of Woolf's birth in 1982 (Ginsberg and Gottlieb, 1983, pp. 1–10), and the feminist critic Carolyn Heilbrun (Heilbrun, 1988, pp. 80–1), tried to reinstate a more moderate understanding of the Woolf marriage.

What is happening here is that Virginia Woolf is being invented anew by partisans of different ideologies. And *To the Lighthouse* has been re-read, not so much as part of a redefined tradition of women's writing, but rather as evidence in the construction of a legend.

It has been taken in evidence by writers primarily investigating Woolf's mental state, including Claire Kahane, who described it as representing, mainly through Lily, Woolf's need to create a unified psyche, and Shirley Panken, who wrote a full-length book describing Woolf's novels as her means of filling her need for maternal love and of mourning her parents.

It has also been used as evidence in some biographies. Roger Poole deduces from Mr Ramsay both Woolf's ambivalent memories of her father (pp. 7–20), and what she came to associate with masculinity during her marriage to the ultra-rationalist Leonard, who, Poole thinks, drove her to madness by insisting that anything that did not meet his standards of rational statement was necessarily untrue (Poole, 1978, pp. 59–73). Phyllis Rose read the novels in conjunction with the newly published autobiographical *Moments of Being*, and took *To the Lighthouse* as directly representing Woolf's memories of her mother. She sees Lily as Woolf's expression of a deep ambivalence towards Julia Stephen. Lily, Rose argues, asserts not only Woolf's need for self-reliance and the ability to refuse to serve other's needs at their whim, but also the guilt involved in this apparent selfishness and the fear that a woman who refuses to be kind is unwomanly and therefore despicable. Mrs Ramsay, who subordinates herself to the needs of others, induces this guilt, and represents Woolf's relationship to the memory of her mother (Rose, 1978, pp. 153–73). A similar reading had been offered the year before by Sara Ruddick, also writing with knowledge of the papers that became *Moments of Being*.

Other critics have seen *To the Lighthouse*, as Leavis did, as a portrait of Sir Leslie Stephen. Morris Beja's *Casebook* even opens with studies of Sir Leslie by other authors, apparently put there for comparison and as valuable material for the reader of the novel (Beja, 1970, pp. 35–55); and at a centenary celebration in 1982 John Harvey described it as a portrait of the father Woolf had carried in her imagination over the years (Warner, 1984, p. 125). Another recent essayist, John W. Bicknell, has attempted to elide Mr Ramsay with stories of Sir Leslie Stephen's youth (Marcus, 1987a, pp. 52–67).

Others have seen in the novel an expression of what they take to have been Woolf's idea of androgyny when she wrote *A Room of One's Own*. Herbert Marder in *Feminism and Art* (published in 1968), a book which predates contemporary feminism, understood feminism and androgyny to mean the abolition of sexual difference. His argument is that Mrs Ramsay is an ideal female, a mother, who is constantly threatened by disruptive forces, especially the enmity between James and his father, and who repeatedly rescues her charges from themselves. Her influence is finally accepted and valued by the males when Mr Ramsay steps ashore at the lighthouse (Marder, 1968, pp. 146–50). Nancy Topping Bazin also understands androgyny as the abolition of difference, and reads *To the Lighthouse* as articulating Woolf's association of some mental qualities with masculinity and some with femininity, an association seen as deriving from Woolf's experience of her parents and of her own manic-depression (Bazin, 1973, pp. 4–20). Lily is seen as representing Woolf's own desire, her effort to balance opposing shapes and harmonise them into an androgynous whole (Bazin, 1973, pp. 44–5, 124). However, the feminist critic Carolyn Heilbrun understands 'androgyny' as a word indicating equality and reconciliation between the sexes, which she sees as the only hope for society and individuals (Heilbrun, 1973, pp. ix–xi). She reads *To the Lighthouse* as culminating in a vision of achieved androgyny when Cam and James, in the boat, accept multiple images of the island and the lighthouse. She argues that neither gender is offered as an ideal without the other: although Mrs Ramsay nourishes others she damages them by protecting them from

the truth, as when she uses her shawl to conceal the skull in
the children's room; and the hell of 'Time Passes' includes
death from both childbirth and the war made by men
(Heilbrun, 1973, pp. 160–3).

These various readings, feminist and other, of Woolf's life
in the novel, have of course also generated particular
readings of the novel itself. There is, however, an unresolved problem about how to read this or any other novel in
the light of a belief that it is in some specific way
autobiographical.

If this involves comparing the novel directly with other
written material provided by the author, such as diary
entries, the exercise is at least clearly defined. Jean Guiget's
Virginia Woolf and her Works (1965) was an explicit attempt
to increase understanding of both Virginia Woolf and her
novels by relating them to the parts of her diaries made
available in *A Writer's Diary*. The discussion of *To the
Lighthouse* uses Woolf's references to the writing of the novel
in her diary, and shows how the project evolved from an
initial idea about her father alone in a boat into something
wider in scope, involving both her memories of her mother
and her love for women friends (Guiget, 1962, pp. 248–60;
reprinted Beja, 1970, pp. 231–45).

How, though, can the reader's knowledge that the novel
involved, for its author, the verbalising of personal memories, help that reader? Often such knowledge is simply
invoked to justify or explain, after the event, conclusions the
reader has come to while reading the novel. For example,
Ian Gregor once argued that the novel is structurally flawed
because Woolf was trying to do two different things, recreate her parents and write a fiction about the emergence of
an artist (Gregor, 1978, pp. 375–89). Gregor's problem is
that he wants the end of the novel to be a climax, a
conclusion, and finds it to be only a stopping (p. 387); and
he deflects the blame for this disappointment on to Woolf,
instead of considering why he wanted a climax.

Much, though not all, feminist discussion of the novel
also uses its definition as autobiography to justify particular
readings after the event. Unease about the activity is
admitted by Gayatri C. Spivak in her 'Unmaking and
Making in *To the Lighthouse*' (1980). Spivak's article is

comparable with the later one by Hillis Miller in that it sees 'Time Passes' as reflecting on the nature of language, of thinking, itself; but it is different in that Spivak attempts to explain this by using knowledge of Woolf's own life, specifically her madness. Spivak, perhaps alone among critics who invoke the author's life, admits she does not know how to insert that life into a text; but she decides to offer her reading without theoretical justification (p. 315).

Spivak proposes that the novel be seen as being about the attempts of Mr Ramsay the thinker and Lily the artist to define or describe Mrs Ramsay. She argues that 'The Window' offers a picture of Mrs Ramsay within marriage, and that 'The Lighthouse' then shows two attempts to find out how to think of her, to represent her, outside that context (pp. 310–11).

She proposes a concept from grammar and logic, that of the 'copula', the link (for example 'is') between the subject and the predicate of a statement, to describe 'Time Passes'. So the form of the novel is: the subject Mrs Ramsay – 'Time Passes' – the representation of Mrs Ramsay; and the crux of the novel is the questioning of that link and so of the very act of representation, of thinking *about* something. Spivak's argument is that in 'Time Passes' the possibility of that link between a subject and its representation is almost denied; and that there the novel seeks, not the definition of a link between life and its representation, Mrs Ramsay and images of her, but a disruption of this familiar way of thinking and an embodiment of the language of madness (p. 311).

In relating the novel to questions about representation, Spivak is claiming it as part of the feminist enterprise of considering the nature of language itself, and its role in determining gender. But in seeing the text itself as a representation of something else, of Woolf's madness, she is actually reinstating the simpler assumption that language imitates that which already exists. The problem about reconciling the feminist pursuit of an existing but obscured female tradition, existing in the lives and work of women in the past, with the feminist investigation of language itself, remains.

Something of a solution, but only for a particular case, is offered by Gillian Beer in her essay 'Hume, Stephen, and

Elegy in *To the Lighthouse*' (1989). This excellent essay centres on a comparison of aspects of *To the Lighthouse* with Sir Leslie Stephen's *English Thought in the Eighteenth Century* (2 vols, 1876). This comparison enables Beer to base a discussion of the presence of Woolf's father in the text of the novel on something more than the bland assumption that Mr Ramsay resembles him. Specifically it establishes Stephen's interest in the philosopher David Hume, and shows Ramsay as sharing this.

Ramsay remembers an anecdote about Hume being stuck in a bog (*TtL*, p. 62). Moreover, Stephen described Hume's philosophical position as a conviction that the history of philosophy is a history of attempts to separate the object and the subject, a clear link with Andrew's description of his father's work (*TtL*, p. 26; Beer, 1989, p. 184). Beer also observes other detailed parallels between *To the Lighthouse* and Stephen's actual exposition of Hume. These include a preoccupation with fame and its survival, and with the relationship between great thinkers and common people, and with the idea of reality as existing only in the varying consciousness of observers (Beer, 1989, pp. 188–91). They also include Hume's use of the example of a table to pose the question as to whether an object exists outside the mind of the observer, and Stephen's use, in expounding Hume, of the images of a man, a tree, a stone, a house, all important images in *To the Lighthouse* also (Beer, 1989, pp. 191–4).

The point of Beer's article is not simply that it establishes a substantial link between the novel and Woolf's father. It uses this knowledge to generate an understanding of the novel which combines a theory about its significance for Woolf herself with a post-structuralist interpretation of its major themes. The article should be read in full. But, summarised briefly, its main argument is as follows. The novel is concerned, like many of Woolf's, with absence. It is centrally concerned, however, with disputing the reality of the separation between subject and object, between thinker or observer and the person or object that is thought about. It therefore disputes the very concept of absence, since that concept depends on a belief in the separation of, the difference between, subject and object: a thing is absent only if its presence in the thoughts of the subject is not real, and only if it has an existence independent of perceptions of it.

The portrayal of Mr Ramsay brings into direct focus the debate about the existence or otherwise of an object without a perceiver. It does so through Ramsay's anxiety about how long his books, or any books, will last (*TtL*, p. 99; Beer, 1989, p. 186). It does so through his chuckling at the thought of Hume stuck in a bog. This follows closely, in the narration of the novel, on his wife's involuntary assertion of the existence of God – 'We are in the hands of the Lord' (*TtL*, p. 61) – and so of existence independent of human observation; it is interrupted, and only resumed once Ramsay is confident of the approval of the world, and so feels free to identify himself with scepticism and to see Hume's having to recite the Lord's Prayer as comic rather than as a serious threat (*TtL*, pp. 62, 65–6; Beer, 1989, pp. 187–8). It does so when Ramsay, like Stephen, debates the relationship between great ideas and the civilisations they become part of (*TtL*, pp. 43–4; Beer, 1989, pp. 189–91).

But, Beer argues, the novel itself takes the debate further than Stephen himself ever did, through its consideration of the power of symbols in thought, and our reliance on symbols to create our system of values.

She argues that the act of symbolising is central to the way in which language operates to make things appear permanent; and that it makes human beings appear to be at the centre of creation because it makes objects mean, signify, something other than themselves and something which is important to the human thinker, not to the object itself (pp. 195–6). This novel, she says, focuses, as did Stephen's account of Hume, on the ending of confidence in the real centrality of humans. But whereas Stephen looked on to evolutionary arguments, replacing the importance of the individual with the importance of the community or the race, *To the Lighthouse* questions completely any attempt to define a firm and permanent relationship between subject and object, consciousness and experience, humanity and nature. The characters attempt to assert their own permanence, their own existence, the power of their thought and memories, but the narration gradually undermines their claims. At the end, the lighthouse is stripped of all the symbolic meaning they gave it, it is simply a tower; and Lily's picture is simply finished (pp. 196–201).

Beer concludes by citing Lacan's idea that the act of making things signify, symbolise, represents an acknowledgement of the power of the father (Beer, 1989, pp. 201–2). In removing her characters and text from the desire to symbolise, Woolf is perhaps removing them from obedience to patriarchy, and herself from obedience to her own father.

With this suggestion Beer's essay specifically relates itself to the concerns of feminist theory, and without simply asserting that the novel represents the memories of its author. Louise DeSalvo's recent *Virginia Woolf: The Impact of Childhood Sexual Abuse on Her Life and Work* (1989), however, demonstrates that a more naive method of relating fiction and biography persists; here the novels are again read so as to reconstruct the story of Woolf, and the scene between the Ramsays at the end of 'The Window' is taken as direct evidence of memories of Leslie Stephen reading aloud from *The Antiquary* (DeSalvo, 1989, pp. 222–7).

Theories of Femininity

Feminist critics have established themselves as rescuers of other women. They seek out women writers whose works were suppressed, they object to repressive stereotypes and role models, they re-read women's writings so as to show the resistance to patriarchal structures within them. This is often very exciting, very enlightening for women readers, and sometimes very brave. But it often constructs the critic as a person of knowledge, a separate observer of the struggle being described. It sometimes perpetuates the situation described in this book, whereby the critic may discuss the theory of the end of any belief in the separation of the observer and the observed, but will still take on the role of detached observer in order to explain this theory. The irony of this for feminist criticism which aspires to deconstruct authority should be obvious, but feminist critics have by no means solved the difficulty.

A brief account of some attempts at a feminist reading of *To the Lighthouse* made over the last two decades will demonstrate the problem.

Early on, there were complaints that the political consciousness of *A Room of One's Own* and *Three Guineas* did not sufficiently suffuse the novel. Kate Millett's *Sexual Politics* complained that Woolf glorified two housewives in Mrs Dalloway and Mrs Ramsay and was unsuccessful in portraying the woman artist's frustration in Lily (pp. 139–40). Patricia Stubbs complained at greater length later, saying that in spite of her polemical essays Woolf was more interested in aesthetic experiment than in combating the idea of women embodied, for example, in Lawrence's novels (pp. 225–35). Even recently, Pamela Transue has argued that Woolf's feminism is only latent in her novels (pp. 1–16), and her reading of *To the Lighthouse* compares it with *Mrs Dalloway* very conventionally as a series of portraits of characters drawn from Woolf's own life (pp. 65–110). Another earlier feminist critic, Ellen Moers, saw more ambivalence in Woolf's portrayal of homebound middle-class housewives (p. 237); but Moers' position is still that of an enlightened observer viewing the content of the novel from a secure position. None of these critics asks any question about how a woman might read the text; all assume reading is unproblematic, and that a feminist reading is a search for a feminist political message in the contents of the novel.

More recently critics have discerned, not feminist polemic, but feminist anxiety in the novel. Their new readings have opened the novel up for many women readers in a most exciting way, making it accessible and fascinating in ways unforeseen even ten years ago. But there must be reservations about even these readings, because although their ideas differ from those of many of the critics I have discussed, their way of reading is still repressive. They are still defining a 'right' conclusion to the experience of reading the novel.

I have already described feminist readings of the novel in terms of the mythology of Demeter and Persephone, which are cases in point. In comparison, Evelyn Haller argues even more dogmatically that Woolf was interested in ancient Egypt and that she repeatedly used the myth of Isis, guardian of the Alexandria lighthouse, to memorialise her own mother. Haller's attention focuses on *Between the Acts* rather than *To the Lighthouse*, however.

More interesting, perhaps, is feminist criticism which invokes recent readings and rereadings of Freud in order to explain gendered behaviour. Central to this criticism, and much disputed in it, is the idea of the Oedipus complex, also invoked by non-feminist critics of the novel to describe James's role. According to common versions of this, young infants do not differentiate between themselves and their mothers, and are not, in psychological terms, gendered. As they achieve separation, conceptualisation of themselves as individual, they encounter gender. Children of both sexes desire their mother at this Oedipal stage; but they observe either their difference from her, their possession of the male sexual organ which she desires, or their lack of that organ. The boy's rivalry with his father for possession of his mother induces fear of retributive castration, but is eventually resolved when he recognises that he too will become a man able to love a woman of his own. The girl, however, perceives herself as already lacking, and as one of the possessed instead of as a possessor. While some feminists reject this account as being based wholly on repressive and arbitrary assumptions about the universal power of masculinity, others, ever since Juliet Mitchell's *Psychoanalysis and Feminism* (1974), have used it as a basis for discussing observable differences between the genders.

An interesting recent example is Rachel Bowlby's discussion of *To the Lighthouse* (Bowlby, 1988, pp. 62–79). She asserts Woolf's knowledge of Freud's work (pp. 65–6), and applies Freudian ideas of gender-identity to the text. As part of a metaphor on which her whole book is based, she likens the feminine to a scene viewed from a moving train, looked back to rather than looking, and excluded from the train; and the masculine to the watching passenger, looking back as if at his mother but with fantasies also of progress (p. 66).

Mr Ramsay desires, of course, to reach his destination, comically represented as R, or even Z; but he also needs to remake, through his wife, his pre-Oedipal union with his mother. Charles Tansley needs her for this purpose too, pouring out his childhood to her. James, meanwhile, resents his father's intrusion on the relationship between him and his mother (Bowlby, 1988, pp. 66–70). As Bowlby says,

Freud indicated that while a woman may attract a man because he sees his mother in her, it is usually only his son who gets that maternal relationship with her! So the man and the woman are in different stages of psychological life at the one time (p. 68).

For the woman, meanwhile, the progress to identity is even more problematic, for the female is defined, by women as by men, both as that which is looked back at and idealised, the imagined mother, and as that which is stupid for not being masculine. Mrs Ramsay seems to others like the ideal imagined mother. But, as Bowlby makes clear, to herself she seems threatened by life, and to be able only to cover and hide discord, not to resolve it (Bowlby, 1988, pp. 71–3). Moreover Lily, so often read as the antithesis of Mrs Ramsay, is analogous to her. Both try to create unity and harmony, in life or in art, and both fail – for Lily's picture, like Mrs Ramsay's soothings, really only serves to emphasise the absence of that unity (Bowlby, 1988, pp. 73–4).

So Bowlby sees the novel as representing the dangers of the prevailing stereotypes of both genders, the hero and the angel in the house: both roles are contradictory and so ultimately untenable, but men and women try to act them out. And she uses Freudian ideas to describe those stereotypes and their origins.

This reading involves a way of thinking about the novel which has been disgracefully absent from almost all criticism of it: it involves considering Mrs Ramsay as a character with her own subjectivity, her own consciousness, not just as a person thought about by the other characters. Even in most feminist criticism this does not happen. But Bowlby's reading, interesting though it is, still involves imposing apparently objective ideas on to the text so as to define it from a position of authority.

The work of Nancy Chodorow is cited by various critics who want to trace in the novel, not the glories of motherhood and wifehood, but the difficulties female children experience in separating themselves from their mothers into fully independent personalities. Chodorow's work is not a repetition of Freud's, but indicates that the practice of giving mothers sole control over the care of infants involves children in a struggle to achieve their separation from her;

and that this is ultimately harder for girls, who cannot see themselves as different from her, and who develop less of a sense of a difference between themselves and other people than do boys (e.g. Chodorow, 1979, pp. 258–62).

For example, Joan Lidoff claims that *To the Lighthouse* really creates a feminine voice, and a new female genre; and that it does this by being permeated in both language and meaning with an awareness of union, of lack of separation, which Lidoff relates to Chodorow's account of a girl's relationship with her mother (pp. 43–5).

Carolyn Heilbrun also proposes a new reading that would substitute the story of mother and daughter, of their difficult development from fusion to separation and mutual respect, for the familiar reading of the model wife and mother whom everyone adores. She identifies three daughters in this telling: with Lily as daughter-figure she compares Prue and Cam. Lily's story is told as that of the daughter who learns that she must find a new way for herself. Prue, of course, is never separate from her mother whom she follows even into death, through childbirth. And for Cam, Heilbrun refers to a fascinating article by Elizabeth Abel (published in the same year, 1987).

This is ' "Cam the Wicked": Woolf's Portrait of the Artist as her Father's Daughter'. Abel uses *A Room of One's Own* as a gloss on the novel, and is concerned principally with the idea of the woman who is struggling to find her way into language. In her reading she relates this idea to the idea that at the Oedipus crisis the male child identifies not only with his particular father but also with the power of language and of rational thought; and that the female child internalises her exclusion from power in language. She draws attention to Cam, whose story dramatises the problems facing a woman who tries to think through the male tradition (p. 172).

Cam in 'The Window' was enigmatic to others, a puzzle even to her mother, and yet seemed wholly in charge of her own affairs (Abel, 1987, p. 173). She could also interpose her own story in that requested by another, when she put her account of the old woman in the kitchen drinking soup before her answer to her mother's question about the return of the walkers (*TtL*, p. 54; Abel, 1987, p. 179). But in 'The

Lighthouse' Cam is passive, contrasted by Abel with James (Abel, 1987, p. 173). At the beginning of the voyage both are angry. But Cam is subordinated by the syntax – 'James thought, and Cam thought' (*TtL*, p. 152); 'So James could tell, so Cam could tell' (*TtL*, p. 153; Abel 1987, p. 173). She is subordinated to male power also by the way she listens to her father and Macalister discussing the winter shipwreck, and imagines others, not herself, in the story; and also by the way she thinks of the pact with James against tyranny as his law (Abel, 1987, pp. 173–5). Just as James's mind flashes back to infancy as he confronts his father, and he half remembers the scene in front of the drawing-room window, so Cam's mind remembers too. But she remembers going out of the garden into her father's study to where the men were reading, and reading about other great men. There she would watch them. And in the boat she still accords them authority: they would have been able to tell her if the island had a place in the universe (*TtL*, p. 175; Abel, 1987, pp. 175–7). She knows the outside of her father's book, but not its contents, its meaning (*TtL*, p. 176; Abel, 1987, p. 180). And as they reach the lighthouse she is a silent follower of the men. Wanting the masculine power in language, she is silenced (Abel, 1987, p. 181).

This seems to me to be a very interesting reading of the novel. But in explaining it Abel is prolonging the ambiguity present in much feminist criticism that draws on readings of Freud. On the one hand it is claimed that a woman is a distinct being, wholly contained within her identity and separate from all other people; that she has her own story within herself, ready to be given form if the appropriate vehicle is to hand; that, like Abel's reading of Cam, she is independent to start with but repressed by the dominance, in language and in institutions, of men. On the other hand, the post-Freudian ideas invoked define the human individual as a process not a distinct being; and as a process in which experience is made conscious, not as itself, but in signs, in language. If one thinks 'I', that 'I' is not oneself, it is a sign standing for oneself. And one can think of oneself only in terms of signs, because as soon as one thinks, one thinks in terms of the signs that are available. So the very idea of the self is made available only by the language. It follows that no individual can be thought of as having a story ready to tell but as lacking the language in which to conceptualise that story. Without the language the story does not exist at all.

The authority most cited for this latter view is the French psychoanalyst Jacques Lacan. At the centre of his ideas as understood by many feminists writing in English is his perception that Freud himself never fully articulated the implications of his own ideas, and his insistence that the process by which a human individual is formed must be rethought. Juliet Mitchell writes that Lacan dedicated himself to making psychoanalysis into an enquiry about the way in which the human subject – the conscious 'I' – is formed. He rejected the humanist idea of the individual as an entity, and posited instead a process in which the infant, at first a formless chaos of experience, learns, not to define its own boundaries, but to conceptualise itself by a constant process of splitting. Consciousness itself is formed only by a split between experience and the images in which that experience is mirrored. The infant enters language, enters the system of images, when it wants, desires, something not present – its mother when it is hungry, for example. The mother only comes into existence as an object that is thought about, only becomes a sign that is part of the infant's consciousness, when the infant lacks her (Mitchell and Rose, 1982, pp. 4–6).

According to Mitchell, Lacan, like Freud, saw gender distinction as being, not innate and essentially connected to biological characteristics, but created in a stage of the Oedipus complex. Many later writers, including psychoanalysts, had objected to Freud's idea that girls and boys both desire their mothers sexually in infancy and in a 'masculine' way, and that while boys fear castration because of this tabooed desire, girls learn that they must transfer their desire to their fathers, and wait to be loved. Lacan went back to this idea, and made it the key to the understanding both of human sexuality and of the creation of each human's subject-consciousness. He argued, not that an already existing boy feared the loss of his penis, or that an already existing girl discovered her lack of one: but that the infants are made into one gender or the other as they desire the phallus, the instrument of power, and think of it, while desiring their mothers, in the sign of the penis which they either possess or lack (Mitchell and Rose, 1982, pp. 5–7).

The significance of this is that it makes the construction of gender inseparable from the acquisition of, or entry into, language. A speaking or thinking human subject is necessarily constructing himself or herself either as possessing the sign of that which is desired, or as debarred from possessing it. This means that both possession and non-possession, equated with masculinity and feminity, are experienced by all humans to varying extents. It also defines femininity as that which is powerless, that which is silenced. Hence its attraction to critics who want to describe the silencing of women.

But their enterprise involves equating the idea of pre-existing defined individuals, permanently and socially female, who, for social, economic, or religious reasons have been deprived of access to writing, with the idea of a determining aspect of all human thinking.

Patricia Waugh seems to have argued recently that the two positions can be reconciled. For example, Waugh says that as women realise they have been traditionally constructed, by everyone including themselves, as objects, as the 'other' they will necessarily, at first, desire to construct themselves as female; and that the Lacanian idea of identity as a process of signs will be pursued by feminists, but only after the female subject position has been established (Waugh, 1989, pp. 6–16). However, this indicates that women exist independently and can choose to construct themselves as they wish; and it is therefore at variance with the Lacanian idea which is nevertheless invoked, that culture-systems define the individual.

In her discussion of *To the Lighthouse* (pp. 108–15) Waugh argues that this novel is itself an attempt, by Woolf, both to reveal the lack of a feminine subject-position and to create one. The form of the novel, which Waugh still sees as including recurring symbolic echoes, an absence of plot, and the lack of an omniscient narrative authority, is said to lack autonomous focus and so to express the feminine voice. This voice is defined, with reference to Chodorow, as relational rather than independent, as depending on other things for definition (p. 108). Lily's story, however, dramatises the struggle between the desire for oneness with the mother, Mrs Ramsay, and the desire for independence, for autonomy (p. 109). Her attempt to recover Mrs Ramsay in her painting is seen as an attempt to recover a lost imaginary fusion; but she completes her painting only when she no longer wants Mrs Ramsay. She has to choose between alienation from the imagined state of unity if she opts to take on a system of signs by constructing a painting, or embracing that state and abandoning her painting and, with it, her autonomous existence (p. 113). Waugh claims that Lily resolves the opposition by seeing the necessity for relations to other people – unlike Mr Ramsay in his isolated search for R – and by at the same time maintaining her separation from them, sympathising with Mr Ramsay only when she can praise his boots (p. 115).

This is too easy to be a real solution to the problem. It simply reduces the debate to two ideas, both neatly defined and viewed as objects. They are imposed on the text, like most of the ideas discussed in this section, by an authoritarian reader seeking to impose closure.

The discussion also bypasses the issue formulated by psychoanalysis, the understanding of language and conscious thought as a system that necessarily represses that which is not language: the argument that as soon as a thing is thought of, it is thought of in terms of a sign but is not the thing itself. Waugh constitutes preverbal desire for union with the mother as an idea which can be directly represented in words, ignoring the argument that representation is itself an act of the symbolic order, the system of signs, and cannot, therefore, be a manifestation of the repressed. Other recent feminist critics have sought to resolve this issue by trying to redefine more positively that which Freud and Lacan label the repressed, sometimes by using the work of Julia Kristeva, another psychoanalyst and philosopher working in Paris.

Toril Moi invoked three ideas ascribed to Kristeva in order to try to define Woolf as a feminist. One is Kristeva's suggestion that modernist writing that disrupts logical construction is itself revolutionary. The second is that some women, more than men, are able to let the force of the subconscious disrupt rational language because of their stronger links with the pre-Oedipal mother-image. Such women are in danger, as Woolf perhaps might be seen to have been, of giving in entirely to this chaotic pre-language state and of falling into madness (Moi, 1985, pp. 11–12). (Kristeva herself cited Woolf's suicide as an example of this tendency: Kristeva, 1974a, p. 157.) The third idea, however, is that this revolutionary potential in a person is determined not by biological sex but by the identity in relation to language that has been taken up. Kristeva argues, says Moi, that it must eventually be perceived that all distinctions between masculine and feminine are fictitious; and Moi suggests that Woolf advocates this too, both in Lily's rejection of the polarised roles of the Ramsays for herself and in the concept of androgyny in *A Room of One's Own* (Moi, 1985, pp. 12–13).

It is the second of these ideas, the suggestion that women have a privileged link with the pre-Oedipal, that is most taken up by others. It seems to remove the impossibility of a female subject-position that Lacanian theory insists on: it means there is some knowledge that the feminine consciousness directly articulates.

For example, Makiko Minow-Pinkney cites Kristeva's theory in 'Revolution in Poetic Language' that conscious identity consists, for both sexes, not only of the symbolic, the order of language and signs, but also of the 'semiotic'. This is thought of as existing like a store of rhythms, shapes, colours, that relate to the pre-Oedipal system of communication but do not signify things other than themselves. Kristeva argues that poetic texts articulate the semiotic in tension with the symbolic, and so give expression to both aspects of the consciousness (Minow-Pinkney, 1987, pp. 17–20).

Minow-Pinkney also cites Kristeva's argument in *About Chinese Women* that in western culture a little girl faces a choice between identifying primarily with her mother, and intensifying that which develops in the pre-Oedipal phase, or identifying primarily with her father, in which case she denies the pre-Oedipal in favour of the symbolic. This is taken to mean that a woman cannot fail to have access to both systems, for if she identifies primarily with the pre-Oedipal she still enters the symbolic in order to talk; and if she identifies primarily with the symbolic order, with the power of the father, she is still biologically female. Minow-Pinkney relates this to Woolf's idea that a woman can think back through her mothers or her fathers, and proposes as a major project of her book the tracing of the tension between the two, between Kristeva's symbolic and semiotic, in the novels (pp. 21–3). But her discussion of *To the Lighthouse* (pp. 84–116) is disappointingly familiar, relying largely on reading Mr and Mrs Ramsay as a polarity which opposes literal to metaphorical habits in language, and a reliance on language to a pre-Oedipal identity.

Minow-Pinkney herself acknowledges one problem in Kristevan theory, which is its total lack of engagement with the social experience of females, the roles they occupy because they are women (pp. 20–1). There are other problems too, however. One is the association of the feminine with the lack of power in public discourse, in speech, and also with infancy, mothering, disruptiveness of rational order, and, ultimately, the danger of madness. As many critics have observed, this serves merely to perpetuate dangerous and hurtful stereotypes. Janet Todd, for example, criticises Moi for claiming Woolf as a revolutionary in Kristevan terms by linking her madness, her textual experiments, and her feminism (Todd, 1988, p. 75).

Another, major, problem is the way in which Kristeva's ideas are reduced, like so many other ideas, to an object, which is then imposed on the text by a detached observer. Such criticism becomes another example of imposed closure. This happens in Minow-Pinkney's discussion of *To the Lighthouse*. It also happens when Jane Marcus in 'A Rose for Him to Rifle' equates Mrs McNab with Kristeva's semiotic (Marcus, 1987b, p. 7).

But Marcus herself later begins to use Kristevan ideas to articulate an experience in reading the text. In 'Still Practice, A/Wrested Alphabet: Toward a Feminist Aesthetic' she contrasts the two ways of reading exemplified by Mr and Mrs Ramsay, and concludes that while he reads to define his own identity, she loses hers as she reads, merging with a text (Marcus, 1988, pp. 239–46). Marcus then suggests that most readers find *To the Lighthouse* difficult to dominate rationally, and that they experience a threat of the dissipation of their own identity as they read; and that in the balancing of one kind of reading with the other we are made to experience the limitations of both. The rational reading imposes a repressive order, and the reading which leads back from language to the pre-Oedipal state leads ultimately to the destruction of self (Marcus, 1988, pp. 247–9).

However, the problems remain. Feminist discussion of psychoanalytic theory is sometimes obsessive, and it often coagulates as lumps of exposition that have only very simplistic connections with the texts supposedly being read. Those connections include an uneasy but largely unquestioned equation of 'the feminine' in psychoanalysis with the fact of women characters and a woman author; an easy, even glib, assumption that the woman author has represented the disruptive presence of her femininity in her novel, both in her style and in her subject-matter; and an assumption that the social roles of women are of less interest than the supposedly universal psychic ones.

A final example of this is the work of an American critic, Margaret Homans, who takes *To the Lighthouse* as her starting and finishing points for a study of women as writers of novels, and who uses the work of Lacan and Chodorow and Kristeva to define the anxieties she sees manifested in their novels.

In *Bearing the Word, Language and Female Experience in Nineteenth Century Writing* (1986) she proposes that women writers are deeply affected by the dominance in western culture of myths that associate the acquisition of language with the loss through death or absence of the mother. As examples of such myths she cites not only Freud's reading of Oedipus, but also *Genesis*, *Paradise Lost*, the *Oresteia*, and Wordworth's *The Prelude* (Homans, 1986, pp. 1–5). She uses Lacan's account of language acquisition as a contemporary retelling of this mythology, not as a universal truth; and she indicates her objection to it by using ideas derived mainly from Chodorow.

Briefly she argues that Lacan's account relies on the assumption that children are male. It does so because it actually celebrates the child's perception of the difference between itself and its mother: the perception of a difference, and so of the lack of the mother, that institutes the child's capabilities in the symbolic (Homans, 1986, pp. 5–11).

But if the child is a girl, Homans says, difference is perceived between the child and the father, and so the notion of sexual difference has very different significances (pp. 8–9). She cites Chodorow to explain that the girl's relationship to her mother contradicts, instead of reinforcing, the importance of the substitution of signs for her, because the girl has never been denied possession of the mother (pp. 11–12). She also suggests that this is seen as a disadvantage for the girl only if it is assumed that the male situation, the devotion to signs instead of to the direct experience of the mother, is seen as preferable. Instead, Homans sees the daughter as privileged because she learns to use the symbolic language without losing the presymbolic one (p. 13).

To develop her argument, Homans introduces the scene in *To the Lighthouse*, where Mrs Ramsay soothes Cam by covering the skull in the bedroom with a shawl. Not only does Mrs Ramsay satisfy the contrary demands of both children by leaving the skull there but covering it up, but also she communicates with Cam by using language not figuratively but in a way that Homans describes by means of Kristeva's idea of the semiotic. Mrs Ramsay does not mean to represent actual mountains and so on to Cam, but to reassure Cam simply of her presence (Homans, 1986, pp. 16–18).

Homans goes on (pp. 19–21) to suggest that women writers in general resist writing that, like all novels, uses words as signs, referring to something other than themselves. Her book is taken up with tracing this anxiety in various texts, and she closes it with a 'Postscript', a discussion of *To the Lighthouse* which she labels 'Virginia Woolf's Victorian Novel' (pp. 275–88). Her argument here is that Mrs Ramsay knows both the symbolic and the presymbolic (p. 280); but Cam and Lily are ranged on opposing sides of language, for Cam relates to language non-referentially, liking only the word 'flounder' in James's story (*TtL*, p. 55), and mindlessly repeating her mother's words to herself as she falls asleep in the boat (*TtL*, p. 188; Homans, 1986, pp. 281–4), while Lily still seeks to represent something other than itself in her picture (Homans, 1986, pp. 284–6).

This is ingenious, and it, like Abel's essay, is interesting in its elucidation of Cam. But it is still reductive, as well as obscure. It imposes preformed ideas on the text of the novel in such a way as to remove attention away from the experience of reading it and to substitute for that experience a dogmatic closure. It also assumes the novel has a meaning to be discovered, just as Woolf's biographers assume that there is a real Virginia Woolf to be captured.

PART TWO
APPRAISAL OF THE TEXT
Attempts to Construct a Feminist Reading

A feminist reading should involve constructing the reader, not the text, as female. A text is what the reader makes it.

Feminist readers have not yet really discovered how to do this, as opposed to how to impose on a text readings that are particularly interested in women, or in whatever is defined as feminine. It is important to try, however. If, as we read, we allow ourselves to become detached observers of the feminine, we are making ourselves into something not-feminine. This means we perpetuate the habit within ourselves of regarding that which is feminine as 'other', and as idiosyncratic. It also means we deprive ourselves of the opportunity to articulate our own lives in what we read. It seems to me that so many girls and women choose to study English Literature because they hope, perhaps without realising it, that in that academic subject they will actually be studying their own experience. But they are often disappointed, even in English.

Three brief essays follow here. In each of them I have tried, in a different way, both to use the existing interests of feminist criticism, and to try to construct my own reading identity as a female one. These readings are not meant to contradict any of those described in the rest of this book. They are offered as additional suggestions.

Mrs Ramsay's Story

This essay is fairly conventional, in that it observes a woman character, Mrs Ramsay. But in doing this it defines more closely aspects of the novel which have been ignored; and it picks up these aspects entirely because of my recognition in the novel of images familiar in my own life, which is that of a middle-class English daughter, wife, and mother.

For many years I struggled to read, and teach, *To the Lighthouse* as a modernist text with puzzling narrative strategies and with a historically significant discussion of art. When I realised, quite recently, that I could allow myself to be interested in the affairs of women, the novel appeared transformed. I now find it incredible that so many critics think of it as having no plot. I see 'The Window' as the story of a quarrel between a husband and wife, and 'Time Passes' and 'The Lighthouse' as adjuncts to that story, offering not exactly the sequel but certainly indications of an outcome.

Jane Lilienfeld interestingly described the novel as a portrayal of a Victorian marriage, in which the wife's duty is to serve her husband (Lilienfeld, 1981). I also associate Mrs Ramsay, as have others, with Virginia Woolf's later, and much quoted, description of 'the Angel in the House' in her 1931 essay 'Professions for Women' (Barrett, 1979, pp. 57–63), and *To the Lighthouse* becomes the first of a series of texts in which Virginia Woolf discusses the collusion of women in their own repression.

The angel in the house is a 'phantom', an image of how a woman should be, carried in a woman's mind and inherited, Woolf claims, from the Victorians. She is insistently unselfish, always deferring to the wishes of others, and always colluding to maintain the unchallenged confidence and superiority of men. She never admits, even to herself, the existence of any other desire. Woolf, indeed, claims to have killed this 'phantom' in herself, and suggests that it is perhaps not a problem known by a younger generation; but many readers in the 1990s claim to recognise in this essay a clear image of their own minds still.

Mrs Ramsay is presented at the beginning of the novel in similar terms. As all readers recognise, she is concerned to soothe and please her son James. In the paragraphs that follow she is said to want to ensure the comfort and happiness of all men, including James, including the lighthousekeepers, and including the aggressive Charles Tansley; as having taken 'the whole of the other sex under her protection' (*TtL*, p. 11), and moreover as being anxious to ensure that her daughters learn to think likewise.

Her reasons for 'protecting' men, for taking it upon herself to make them feel happy, are vague:

> she had the whole of the other sex under her protection; for reasons she could not explain, for their chivalry and valour, for the fact that they negotiated treaties, ruled India, controlled finance; finally for an attitude towards herself which no woman could fail to feel or to find agreeable, something trustful, childlike, reverential; which an old woman could take from a young man without loss of dignity, and woe betide the girl – pray Heaven it was none of her daughters! – who did not feel the worth of it, and all that it implied, to the marrow of her bones. (*TtL*, p. 11)

Orlando, published in the following year, is a portrayal of ways in which, throughout English history since the reign of Elizabeth, gender-roles have dominated human social behaviour, to the detriment of both men and women. Above all, women are portrayed as needing to manage men so as to earn their protection. The management is complex: women make themselves both helpless and beautiful, so that men are their bold and admiring rescuers; but because men might be tempted into dangerous escapades by the women, the women themselves have to exercise the responsibility of modesty. Orlando herself, newly become a woman after starting life as a man, works all this out carefully for herself on a voyage home from Turkey; and the rest of the novel bears it out.

Orlando assumes that this state of affairs is universal. In *A Room of One's Own*, however, the economic forces behind the dependence of women on men begin, of course, to be discussed; and in 'Professions for Women' Virginia Woolf tried to make them crucial, claiming, bravely if not convincingly, that the possession of five hundred pounds a year – economic independence – makes it possible for a woman to be free of a dependence on charm for her living.

In *To the Lighthouse*, however, Mrs Ramsay's economic dependence on her husband is barely relevant. The need to provide for his family, to pay for the repairs to the greenhouse roof, are threats to his academic singlemindedness, but do not directly explain her need to ensure his, and all men's, happiness. Mrs Ramsay is perhaps the clearest example in Virginia Woolf's fiction of the female who simply defines herself in terms of the contentment she facilitates in others, especially men.

'The Window' dramatises the foolishness, for both sexes, of a woman's desire to define herself by pleasing others. It does so by presenting a story which starts clearly with a husband and wife in opposition:

> 'Yes, of course, if it's fine tomorrow,' said Mrs Ramsay. . . .
> 'But,' said his father, stopping in front of the drawing-room window, 'it won't be fine.' (*TtL*, p. 9)

Mrs Ramsay's desire for the feeling that everyone else is happy is demonstrated further in the following pages, which describe her efforts to cheer up Charles Tansley, whom she regards as 'odious' (*TtL*, pp. 11 and 19). The effects of this on her family are demonstrated too, when her older children are remembered as disappearing 'as stealthily as stags' as soon as dinner is over, in order to find a little privacy for a dispute (*TtL*, p. 13). This compares with the description of the dinner-party at the end of 'The Window', so often read as a triumph for Mrs Ramsay, but inducing horror in me as I read. I am horrified because it so clearly matters to Mrs Ramsay that guests and family should cohere into a group in which everyone is pleased; but in wanting this she is wanting something that over-rules everybody else. She has 'triumphed' (*TtL*, p. 69) over William Bankes's preference for privacy; her triumph is endangered by the lateness of Paul and Minta, though restored by their obedience in becoming engaged; her triumph is endangered also by her guests at the meal, by Lily's short-lived resistance to Charles Tansley, by her husband's reaction to Carmichael's request for soup. Her triumph is tawdry anyway because, as Charles Tansley rightly thinks early on (*TtL*, p. 80), the conversation is feeble, 'damned rot'. The one certain triumph is the food: it is the one thing with which she pleases Augustus Carmichael, and Bankes himself applies the word 'triumph' to the beef (*TtL*, p. 93). But Mrs Ramsay has not cooked the food herself, only supervised others. All this appals me, not only because Mrs Ramsay is tyrannical to others, as many have observed, but also because for Mrs Ramsay failure is inevitable. The roles of wife, mother, housewife, beautiful woman, and ensurer of good cheer are impossible to succeed in, when they assume that all responsibility belongs to the woman, and that no one else can take responsibility for him or herself. Everyone else, of course, except the children Cam and James, does in fact take responsibility for his or her own desires, in spite of Mrs Ramsay.

The result of this situation is that Mrs Ramsay is easily weary, discouraged; and, because she is apparently so good, she induces guilt in others when they cannot play the parts she wants for them.

We have no real evidence that Mr Ramsay is right about the weather, except his image of himself as someone who insists on truth. He insists on truth no more than anyone else. He also knows (*TtL*, p. 34) that it might in fact be fine tomorrow. The opening dispute between the Ramsays is more easily read as an example of her need to please, and of his exasperation at that and at all it involves.

After some pages, and a few minutes in the 'present time' of the story, Mr Ramsay sees Mrs Ramsay still knitting the stocking for the lighthousekeeper's boy and still allowing James to hope the trip to the lighthouse will take place. He stamps in irritation at her and says 'Damn you' (p. 34). She, faced with his displeasure which means he is not happy, gives in in silence, reassures him that he need not go to the coastguards for an authoritative opinion of the weather and that his word on the subject is enough, and never mentions it again. The principle is clear. She is the one who gives way. In doing so, of course, she reasserts, and compounds, her identity as the comforter. So the opposition between their roles is confirmed.

Soon the child is taken away to be put to bed and Mrs Ramsay sinks into a private silence. Her husband sees her and, in spite of his desire to speak with her, refrains from interrupting her solitude; but she, apparently knowing his desire, gives way to him again, interrupts her own reverie and joins him in walking in the garden. This walk, however, does not resolve their separation, their opposition. His irritation, his 'Damn you', is not mentioned. Instead, he adopts a series of poses – that of pessimist about the world, that of her passionate admirer, that of admirer of her flowers – and she knows, allowing herself no rancour, that these are only poses. So they continue in their opposed roles, she as the one who tries to make others happy, he as the difficult one. There is no dialogue of equals.

In the dinner party that follows they are separated from each other by the length of the table and by their different desires – his that he should not be bored, hers that people should warm to her and to each other. Each of them is separately helped into a contented mood by some of their guests, not by each other.

Finally they are alone together, reading. Gradually their attention leaves their books and turns to each other. She wants him to speak to her, but he, still self-assertive, likes to watch her silent beauty as she reads. So she gives way and speaks first, and they exchange pleasantries which lead to his assertion that she won't finish the stocking she is still knitting for the lighthousekeeper's son. She agrees. Then he, she perceives, wants her to speak, to say how she loves him. She doesn't speak, since he is the assertive one with power in speech; but soon she turns to look at him and 'The Window' ends with her submission, for what she does say is 'Yes, you were right. It's going to be wet tomorrow.' (*TtL*, p. 114).

The narrator's voice at this point comments 'She had not said it, but he knew it. And she looked at him smiling. For she had triumphed again.'

She has 'triumphed', presumably, because amity is supposedly restored between them. But this triumph is not achieved through a resolution of their difference, their opposition. There is no synthesis. It is achieved only through her submission to him, her confirming that he is wise. It is therefore just a reaffirming of her role as bringer of pleasure, and of his as the person who should be pleased. Read this way, 'The Window' is the story of an impossible relationship in which both are caught. The woman must please: the man must be pleased, and is to blame if he is not pleased by her.

The other two sections of the novel give accounts of the consequences of the situation. Mrs Ramsay submits completely; she dies. With her death the family falls apart, both actually in that other members of it die too, and metaphorically in that their house, the place where she operated her soothing functions, is abandoned and falls into near ruin. Eventually, however, the remaining family returns and starts up again without her. But nothing is changed. Mr Ramsay makes the trip to the lighthouse after all, but does so through guilt at not having done what his unselfish wife wanted, and in a way that relies on the willingness of women to help him be happy.

The attempted resistance of both the children and Lily is of no consequence. Cam's silence and Lily's picture impress no one else in the book. They do not even impress me as I read: Cam is repressed, Lily says she has had her vision, not that she has a vision. As alternatives to Mrs Ramsay's desperate situation they offer only loneliness and incoherence. Moreover Lily's story of Paul and Minta as good friends now that Paul has a lover elsewhere (*TtL*, pp. 160–2) only offers an alternative that also excludes a sexual relationship between a man and a woman.

It is easy to say women should not collude, should not build their lives on the desire to please others. But how? Within marriage, the novel offers nothing.

Disintegration of Self

This essay attempts to use ideas derived from the work of Julia Kristeva in order to explain another understanding of Mrs Ramsay. It hopes also to indicate, however, that this use of her work has been repudiated by Kristeva, and that it leads the critic, and perhaps the novel, into an uncomfortable situation.

Early in the novel (*TtL*, pp. 19–20) Mrs Ramsay's soothing work is briefly interrupted. After the first conversation about the weather Mr Ramsay and Charles move on and she settles to comforting and encouraging James; but her careful search for pictures for him to cut out is interrupted when her mind switches to the sound of the waves. Sometimes, we are told, this sound signifies to her the comforts of infancy, recovered for her by becoming a mother herself:

> seemed consolingly to repeat over and over again as she sat with the children the words of some old cradle song, murmured by nature, 'I am guarding you – I am your support' (*TtL*, p. 20).

but at other times it signifies the inevitability of death:

> like a ghostly roll of drums remorselessly beat the measure of life . . . (*TtL*, p. 20)

Her mind switches to this sound from the present task because the men have stopped talking.

It is easy to associate this with Kristeva's idea of what happens to a woman when the symbolic order gives way in her – as it does here when the men stop talking and her attention, held steady by them, lurches away from her job of finding something for James to do. When the symbolic order gives way a woman can either take pleasure by identifying with her mother and feeling herself to be the repressed sublime union; or she can fall apart, die, from the loss of the system that has given her security, especially if her union with her mother was insufficient in the first place (Kristeva, 1974a, p. 150).

In this case, the symbolic order reasserts itself in her almost at once as Mrs Ramsay hears her husband's voice again, even though Ramsay is only chanting Tennyson's poem to himself, not using language as a system of communication.

When James is taken away to bed Mrs Ramsay begins again to withdraw from language. Section 11 (*TtL*, pp. 60–3) can be read as a clear account of this, though with one proviso. This is that it does not actually describe Mrs Ramsay sinking into a pre-Oedipal state, a thing which must by definition be impossible to describe in words; what it does do is describe Mrs Ramsay thinking about herself sinking into a preverbal state.

The scene is clearly constructed, with the narrator moving between formal reporting of her thoughts and the closer integration of narrator and character in free indirect discourse. We hear her relief at not having to talk any more, because of having to be so careful what she says to children – an anxiety that shows her fear of language itself, perhaps. She prefers, it seems, to be silent and solitary, an invisible 'wedge-shaped core of darkness', to become a self that seems 'free' and 'limitless'. Then we hear:

> And to everybody there was always this sense of unlimited resources, she supposed; one after another, she, Lily, Augustus Carmichael, must feel, our apparitions, the things you know us by, are simply childish. Beneath it is all dark, it is all spreading, it is unfathomably deep; . . . (*TtL*, p. 60)

The 'she supposed' not only distances the narration from Mrs Ramsay, but also makes it clear that while she is thinking about an experience outside signifying language, she is still herself actually thinking within language.

As she thinks, however, the narration seems to indicate that she is getting closer to losing thought. The tag 'she thought' is omitted from the following sentences, while the thinking narrator is at the same time clearly marked as separate from her by the ability to observe the cleverness of her knitting:

> Not as oneself did one find rest ever, in her experience (she accomplished here something dexterous with her needles), but as a wedge of darkness. Losing personality, one lost the fret, the hurry, the stir; and there rose to her lips always some exclamation of triumph over life when things come together in this peace, this rest, this eternity; (*TtL*, p. 61)

But the exclamation of triumph – a triumph parallel to her triumphs at disarming her husband and William Bankes? – is not perhaps quite reached. At this point she stops the retreat into darkness and finds, instead, a signifier, and so constitutes her identity again within the symbolic system:

> and pausing there she looked out to meet that stroke of the Lighthouse, the long steady stroke, the last of the three, which was her stroke, for watching them in this mood always at this hour one could not help attaching oneself to one thing especially of the things one saw; and this thing, the long steady stroke, was her stroke. (*TtL*, p. 61)

From this point on she moves quickly back to language and at the end of the paragraph finds herself not only speaking, but speaking words signifying a very patriarchal order of thought, Christianity – 'We are in the hands of the Lord.'

Annoyed with herself for this, she is nevertheless firmly conscious within language now, sorry about the troubles of humans. She has abandoned an approach back to the pre-Oedipal; but within language she is relatively helpless, unable to change the world, and comforts herself, powerless as she is, with a non-signifying delight in the light of the lighthouse beam on the sea, an image that might well be compared with Kristeva's idea of the semiotic, the store within consciousness of non-figurative experience (Kristeva, 1974b, pp. 93–8). Then finally, the narration moves to Mr Ramsay watching her, seeing in her a different and unreachable mode of existence from his own; but she abandons that mode, gets up, and joins him in his as they walk together, talking.

Read this way, Mrs Ramsay is seen as an example of Kristeva's idea that for a woman it might be possible to maintain within consciousness both reason, order, a personal identity within the symbolic order, and also a 'truth' that signifies nothing but itself, an echo of union with her mother, a 'truth' that undermines and is in term repressed by language (Kristeva, 1974a, pp. 152–6).

It is possible to suggest that other characters within the novel need her as representing the possibility of this dual consciousness, which they lack – all, perhaps, except the poet Augustus Carmichael, who manifestly does not need her and who himself seems to occupy a consciousness outside a system of speech and communication. Kristeva has associated poets as well as women with the semiotic consciousness in 'Revolution in Poetic Language' (Kristeva, 1974b).

The story of the dispute between the Ramsays can be read in these terms, and becomes the story of the relation of the man and the woman to the repressed self. As Mr Ramsay approaches her in the section I have just discussed, thinking of Hume stuck in a bog, she is in her withdrawn, semiotic, consciousness; to him she is, at this moment, especially beautiful; but she also seems especially separate, and somehow forbidden, tabooed (*TtL*, p. 63). She initiates the communication between them but does it in his terms, in terms of words representing things, the gardener, Jasper's habit of shooting birds. The conversation is polite. Throughout the next section, Section 12 (*TtL*, pp. 63–8), they remain separate, standing together, even touching, but still separate. He cannot enter her love of the star and flowers, and can only impose himself on the beauty of the place in words – 'Poor little place' (p. 66).

This situation is presented again in the final section of 'The Window' (*TtL*, pp. 108–14). They sit together in the room, he re-reading the work of Scott and she withdrawing into fragmentary, perhaps semiotic, pleasures from a book of poems. Then he watches her, again sees her as beautiful, and also as brainless (pp. 111–12). Again, as before, she responds to his presence, his gaze, by entering into polite ritualistic conversation, and they discuss the engagement of Minta and Paul (p. 112). But on this occasion it is made clear that she wants him to stave off her 'darkness', and to dominate her:

> Do say something, she thought, wishing only to hear his voice. For the shadow, the thing folding them in was beginning, she felt, to close round her again. Say anything, she begged, looking at him, as if for help. (*TtL*, p. 113)

At first he continues silent, but the narrator tells us that in their increasing 'intimacy' she is aware of his increasing dominance over her mind.

When he does speak it is forbiddingly:

> 'You won't finish that stocking tonight,' he said, pointing to her stocking. That was what she wanted – the superiority of his voice reproving her. (*TtL*, p. 113)

And she agrees with him. She has again returned to the symbolic consciousness, to words, and this time with his help. She even repudiates her knitting, a semiotic activity.

He now, she is aware, wants her to tell him she loves him in his language, in words. She cannot do this. Instead she uses words ritualistically, and 'triumphs' because he knows she loves him without her having to represent this in words (*TtL*, p. 114).

The story of their dispute is now one of her desire for the semiotic, the non-symbolic, her guilt, even fear, about it and frequent willingness to abandon it for the symbolic, and her eventual assertion of it in opposition to the male demand for words signifying something other than themselves. Mr Ramsay, meanwhile, desires her beauty when she has withdrawn from language, but can only appropriate her in speech, which drags her away from it.

For other characters too, Mrs Ramsay is a sign of that which they cannot otherwise conceptualise. To Prue, soon to die in childbed, she suddenly represents, signifies 'my mother' (*TtL*, p. 107). And to Lily also she represents that which is repressed by representation. In this Kristevan reading Lily's picture is not, as to so many critics, a mark of her achievement in finding an image of her independent life. Instead Lily is read as moving away from a consciousness that admits only signs – the Ramsays as a symbol of 'marriage' (*TtL*, p. 69), her attempt to use formal shapes to represent Mrs Ramsay – to a consciousness that also knows the semiotic. She learns to make her picture not a sign of that which is absent, Mrs Ramsay on the step, but itself something which is present and not therefore in need of representation, 'that very jar on the nerves, the thing itself before it has been made anything' (*TtL*, p. 178). The reappearance to her of Mrs Ramsay on the step (*TtL*, p. 186) makes perfect sense as an image for us of Lily's reawakened knowledge of the preverbal, of union with a mother. Immediately she also wants Mr Ramsay 'as if she had something she must share', for she also occupies the symbolic order. But her picture is semiotic, is just a line.

This is all very neat, and it has surprised me as I have worked it out. But it makes me uneasy, as being in a sense arbitrary, a reading tried out because some of Kristeva's ideas are fashionable, and yet offered as truth. Moreover, it is yet another closing interpretation forced on the text after many readings, to make it mean something. Like Lily, what I really want to do is to capture the jar on the nerves of actually reading the novel.

But these Kristevan ideas do help to do this if I use them to describe the rest of Mrs Ramsay's story, and my own part in it as I read.

In 'The Window' Mrs Ramsay offers an image of the coexistence of the symbolic and the semiotic consciousness to me as well as to the other characters. She is also shown as always having to choose one or the other, as being unable actually to inhabit both simultaneously; and to live in social terms, to communicate as a personality, she has to choose the symbolic. But eventually she chooses the other, she dies – a possibility clearly described by Kristeva for the woman who slips out of the symbolic (Kristeva, 1974a, p. 157). Eventually Lily joins her, not in death, for she still wants both consciousnesses, but in knowledge of the semiotic; and Mr Ramsay, capable only of the symbolic, represents her to himself in his voyage. But before that there is 'Time Passes'.

Obviously 'Time Passes' represents, to the reader, the existence of things which are the things themselves, not signifiers to an onlooker. 'Time Passes' describes things which are simply *there*: spring, autumn, death, regeneration among plants. These things might become signs in the consciousness of a watcher, but the novel openly denies that they do: the only watchers are Mrs McNab and Mrs Bast, perhaps after all, as Jane Marcus suggests in 'A Rose for him to Rifle' (Marcus, 1987b, p. 7), a sign for the semiotic, or at least females who have knowledge of it.

The semiotic cannot be directly represented in the words of a novel, but can make its presence felt by the disruption of those words (Kristeva, 1974b, pp. 113–17). Here the eruption of 'Time Passes' into the narrative has the effect of confusing, disrupting, my reading. In 'The Window' I followed the story. In reading 'Time Passes' I experience, again and again, great uncertainty. I still try to make it 'mean' something, because that is what I expect of a novel; but the activity seems foolish, irrelevant, or even repressive of the words, the sounds, in my head. I can image this feeling to myself by suggesting to myself that, like Mrs Ramsay, I have left the safe world of language in 'The Window', and am somewhere where descriptions are not available. In a way, I re-enact Mrs Ramsay's story.

In 'The Lighthouse' symbolic readings are clearly in order, because of the way, as Mepham showed, the two different stories stand as metaphors each for the other. In any metaphor, inevitably, one thing signifies another. So, one can argue, we are now made to read consciously within a symbolic system. But this is not much more comfortable than 'Time Passes'. 'The Lighthouse' always seems to me arid and insistent on meaning something other than itself. I look back nostalgically to 'The Window', where, as it now feels, things both were and meant.

The experience of reading *To the Lighthouse* is very much an experience of loss. Thinking about it in Kristevan terms, I see myself as wanting, as I read, both the character of Mrs Ramsay and the richness of 'The Window', which perhaps represents to me the richness of knowing both the symbolic, the power of language, and the semiotic, the memory of union with mother. Neither on its own is welcome.

But I must raise two objections, two 'unwillingnesses', to all this. One is that this means that I, as I read, confirm in myself the gender stereotypes. Not only do I interpret the man, Mr Ramsay, as the chief possessor of the power of language and the signifying system, to be joined of course by James; but also I interpret the females, Mrs Ramsay, Lily, perhaps Mrs McNab and Mrs Bast, *and myself*, a female reader, as those who have knowledge of the preverbal consciousness as well as of the symbolic. This is claimed as a bonus for females by feminist critics using Kristeva's ideas; but it is not a bonus if it invokes death in Mrs Ramsay, solitude and non-communication in Lily, confusion in Mrs McNab, and nostalgia in me. Augustus Carmichael is a male who is apparently endowed with this double knowledge, so the gender association is to that extent undermined; but Augustus is not a figure I wish to follow either. I find in fact that, as with Freud's theory of the Oedipus complex, I must either reject the novel as largely perpetuating an old system of differentiation according to gender, or must accept it as a way of describing something that is unfortunately true: that femininity means instability.

The second objection is this: Kristeva herself has repudiated the 'religion' of feminism, which is both the application of her theories as if they were received truths, and the resulting admiration for the unstable, regarded as feminine (Kristeva, 1979). As Toril Moi indicated, Kristeva looks to a definition of both masculine and feminine as purely metaphysical, separate from the distinction between men and women (Moi, 1986, p. 12). This reading of *To the Lighthouse* in effect ignores that.

But considering it shows up something in the novel, I think: Moi claimed that while Mr and Mrs Ramsay represented the old gender stereotypes, Lily represents the deconstruction of this opposition between masculinity and femininity, and the attempt to construct a new identity; and that *To the Lighthouse* is a feminist novel therefore, not because it admires feminine instability but because it looks for a new idea (Moi, 1986, p. 13). I think Moi is, unfortunately, wrong. I have never been able to take to Lily's loneliness very warmly as a new image of how a woman might be. I now see Lily, instead, as discovering in herself that which Mrs Ramsay also knew. Lily, in fact, confirms the stereotype. The novel confirms it too.

The Narrative Voice Again

This essay attempts to describe the experience of reading *To the Lighthouse* in terms of the reader's relationship to the narrative voice. It is the idiosyncracies of Woolf's narrative voices which, more than anything else, distinguishes her novels. It is also the narrative voice which, as I have argued, puzzled early critics of this novel and led them to search for something more certain, the author in her work, a theme to be defined. Other critics, especially Mepham and Hillis Miller, have done a great deal to describe the workings of the narration. What follows here is an attempt to add to their work a description of the narrative voice itself.

I have a persistent sense as I read many of Woolf's novels that information is being withheld from me by somebody who is telling the story. Moreover, I sense that that somebody is quite a specific personality, but that I am being prevented from unravelling the secret of who it is, and of why she or he is telling me this rather than something else. In this essay I try briefly to define the source of this experience in the text, to consider how it has been related to ideas of Woolf as a modernist, and to consider if it might more sensibly relate to ideas of Woolf as a woman.

I can describe the source of this sense of secrecy in linguistic terms, by discussing the cohesion of particular passages, the extent to which the passage binds, or does not bind, into a coherent whole instead of a series of separate statements or even words. Passages are made coherent by words that refer one part to another, by pronouns, demonstratives, definite articles, and by verbs. Frequently Virginia Woolf's narrators use these referents in an idiosyncratic way; they do not refer to other words within a passage when you expect them to, but sometimes appear to refer outside it. The reader searching for coherence is therefore given the illusion that knowledge external to the passage is being referred to; but that that knowledge, that point of reference, never comes into the passage, is never made explicit. Examples could be given from any novel, but I shall now discuss the opening of *To the Lighthouse*, from the start of the novel to the end of the second long paragraph.

Obviously information is being withheld here. The characters are talking about a visit to a lighthouse, but this information is directly given only later, or is perhaps inferred from the title. Not only is this withholding of information there because we are being given the direct speech of the characters, who know what they are discussing; but also the presence of a narrator is very clear. The narrator has chosen where to start; he or she has also chosen to place the description of James and his reactions between the speeches of his parents, thus creating the effect of a time-lag; and the narrator has chosen to emphasise the parallel between the two opposing opening speeches with the emphatic positioning of the repeated 'But'.

The presence of this narrative voice is largely conventional and unproblematic in the first long paragraph. It has access to the thoughts of both James and Mrs Ramsay, and the transition from one to the other is straightforward: 'he appeared the image of stark and uncompromising severity, . . . so that his mother . . . imagined him'. It is straightforward because the referents are familiar, we know what 'he' and 'his' and 'him' relate to. The clear distinction in the long second sentence between James's activity, which is in the past tense, and the description of the 'great clan', which is a universalising statement in the present tense, does not disrupt the coherence.

In the second long paragraph, however, the cohesion is much more problematic. The second sentence of this paragraph is conventional up to the semi-colon: 'by his mere presence;'. But the section after the semi-colon has no main verb, is not an independent unit. What, then, does it depend on, relate to? Does it relate to the parenthesis '(James thought)'? There is a curious sense to the reader familiar with the book that it might, because the images of knife and blade are ones that James applies to his father later. But that is later, and derives from this episode; so far James's thoughts are apparently on axes and pokers wielded by himself. Moreover the linguistic structure does not support such an interpretation. 'James thought' refers to the verb 'was' in 'who was ten thousand times better', and there is nothing parallel to 'who was' to link 'James thought' with in the rest of this part of the sentence.

So this appears to be, not James, but the narrator: a narrator who hates Mr Ramsay.

Whose thoughts, then, are those in the following sentences – 'What he said was true . . . '? It is likely that these are read as Mr Ramsay's thought, narrated in free indirect discourse in which narrator and character are virtually combined. But then there comes another parenthesis in which the discourse is clearly not Mr Ramsay but a narrator denouncing him, as the word 'little' shows: '(here Mr Ramsay would straighten his back and narrow his little blue eyes upon the horizon)'. Did the narrator's own voice start with the brackets, or was it there in the heavy irony of the earlier phrases, 'the passage to that fabled land where our brightest hopes are extinguished, our frail barks founder in darkness'? I am simply not sure how much of all this is Mr Ramsay and how much is the narrator. My doubt arises because of questions about what the pronouns and verbs relate to, and also because of the effect of irony. The result is crucial to my experience of the novel: I get a clear dislike of Mr Ramsay for the whole novel from here, but I get an equally strong sense that the narrator won't tell me whether he or she is giving me this opinion or whether Mr Ramsay is condemning himself, and is therefore forgivable, even comically directing irony against himself.

Mepham made a similar observation about the ambiguity of a passage later in the novel, and commented on the resulting elusiveness of the narrative voice (Mepham, 1976, p. 157). He relates this elusiveness to the idea of modernism, as did Auerbach before him (Auerbach, 1953, p. 469). They both, instead of, as it were, admitting the elusiveness, construct the idea of a narrative voice that is coherent in a different way. Auerbach sees it as the author herself who chooses to give us not only factual information but also the things she associates with that information (Auerbach, 1953, p. 478); Mepham is concerned to demonstrate that the characters and events of the novel are in fact held in place within a strict narrative structure, by a narrative voice that can simultaneously tell us what a character is thinking and indicate to us how that fits into a scheme that the character would not realistically be aware of. Both see the novel as a kind of jigsaw puzzle into which everything fits neatly; they assume it has a closed form.

I wish, finally, to put this discussion of the novel's narrative voice into the context of feminist criticism, and to do so by raising a number of possibilities which the reader may accept or reject. I do this against the background of the suggestion earlier in this book that Woolf's essay 'Modern Novels' and its successors were part of an unsuccessful attempt to abandon the cohesive narrative voice of Bennett and his contemporaries, and Makiko Minow-Pinkney's perception that this attempt was part of Woolf's feminist resistance to authoritarian forms in the novel (Minow-Pinkney, 1987, pp. 1–23).

Kristeva's theory that the semiotic makes itself known by the disruption of the symbolic order (Kristeva, 1974b, pp. 113–17) could perhaps be invoked again to describe the disruption of a text's cohesion. In that case the construction of a consistent but secretive narrator belongs, not in the text, but in me, in my desire for coherence. According to this argument I, if I am constructing myself as a female reader, should stop myself imposing this coherence and should instead enjoy the text's incoherence. But I object to this, not only because I in fact prefer a novel to be coherent, however much this indicates my own masculine position within the patriarchal symbolic order, but also because, once again, the idea confirms the stereotype of women as chaotic. The answer to that, of course, is that a feminine reading position is not the same thing as a woman, who will necessarily be capable of working within the symbolic order. But still, do I accept the association of femininity with incohesion?

In *A Room of One's Own* Virginia Woolf's persona spoke of the lack of a 'common sentence' suitable for a 'woman's use' in the nineteenth century (p. 73), and of her contemporary Mary Carmichael's having 'broken up' the inherited sentence, but having not yet found how to replace it (p. 87). The idea of a 'woman's sentence' has enticed feminists over recent years. Is Virginia Woolf's narrative voice in *To the Lighthouse* demonstrating a woman's sentence?

I'm not very happy with the idea that sentences indicating an elusive and secretive speaker are female sentences, because, again, the idea simply reinforces a stereotype which I want to repudiate. I can see some kind of argument for it based on the openness of reference, the avoidance of an established 'I', and the possibility of relating this to Lacanian theories connecting the establishment of a definite subject position with masculinity.

The idea of a female sentence may, however, be a digression. Sandra Gilbert has argued (Gilbert, 1987) that Woolf's idea of a woman's sentence does not involve a serious linguistic observation that anyone has ever made, that it is in fact a Utopian metaphor; and she and Susan Gubar have incorporated and elaborated this observation into their recent *No Man's Land* (Gilbert and Gubar, 1988, pp. 227–71). Sara Maitland and Michelene Wandor, in *Arky Types* (1987) which is more a piece of feminist theory than a novel, describe – though the context *might* be ironic – ideas about male sentences being alien to female experience as radical feminist rubbish, confusing use of language with the language itself (Maitland and Wandor, 1987, p. 121); and Deborah Cameron has argued at length in her book (1985) that ideas about language determining the linguistic incompetence of women should be jettisoned.

Perhaps a different kind of suggestion should be made, one that invokes the idea of the author more centrally. Perhaps the secretive narrator represents a version of the situation in the nineteenth century most famously described by Sandra Gilbert and Susan Gubar: that women who wrote defined themselves as seizing the power of the pen from the males, and that they therefore concealed themselves and their opinions within their texts, made them secret from most readers, so as to avoid censure (Gilbert and Gubar, 1979). Perhaps Virginia Woolf, with a Victorian childhood, hid herself, avoided taking up a narrative stance that others could object to? If this is a credible idea, it links with Jane Marcus's reading of *A Room of One's Own* as written in a code that only a few would notice and interpret (Marcus, 1987b, pp. 163–87).

Or perhaps it suggests another way of approaching the issue which avoids inventing Virginia Woolf herself so conveniently: perhaps the narrator of this novel, and the others, and the narrative voice of *A Room of One's Own*, which is composite and elusive as well as possibly speaking in code, and Cam understood as in Elizabeth Abel's reading of her as silenced (Abel, 1987), should all be taken as images created by Woolf of the difficulty women have in writing literature within the existing tradition.

Bibliography

Abbreviations

TtL   *To the Lighthouse*
AROOO   *A Room of One's Own*
Page numbers given for both these texts refer to the Triad Grafton Paperback editions (London), being the most easily available.
Letters Volume 3: Nicolson, Nigel, and Trautmann, Joanne (eds), *A Change of Perspective: The Letters of Virginia Woolf, Volume 3 1923–1928* (London and Toronto, 1977).

Works and Other Writings of Virginia Woolf Referred to in This Book

Books

A Room of One's Own	London 1929
Between the Acts	London 1941
Jacob's Room	London 1922
Mrs Dalloway	London 1925
Orlando, A Biography	London 1928
Roger Fry	London 1940
To the Lighthouse	London 1927

Essays

Mr Bennett and Mrs Brown (London, 1924); first printed as 'Character in Fiction' in *Criterion*, 11, 8 (July 1924); reprinted as 'Character in Fiction' in McNeillie, 1988, pp. 420–38 (see below).

'Mr Bennett and Mrs Brown' (first version), *Nation and Athenaeum* (1 December 1923). This essay, with others following it in *Nation and Athenaeum*, is reprinted in R. Majumdar and A. McLaurin (eds), *Virginia Woolf, The Critical Heritage* (London and Boston, Mass., 1975).

'Modern Novels', *Times Literary Supplement* (10 April 1919); reprinted in McNeillie, 1988, pp. 30–7.

'Modern Fiction', in *The Common Reader* (London, 1925); ed. Andrew McNeillie, 1984, pp. 146–54.

'Professions for Women', a speech given to The Women's Service League in 1931, published in *The Death of the Moth and Other Essays* (London, 1942); reprinted in M. Barrett (ed.), *Virginia Woolf, Women and Writing* (London, 1979).

Other Writings

Bell, Anne Olivier, and McNeillie, Andrew (eds), *The Diary of Virginia Woolf, Volume 3, 1925–30* (London and New York, 1980; Harmondsworth, 1982).

Nicolson, Nigel, and Trautmann, Joanne (eds), *A Change of Perspective: The Letters of Virginia Woolf, Volume 3, 1923–1928* (London and Toronto, 1977).

McNeillie, Andrew (ed.), *The Essays of Virginia Woolf, Volume 3, 1919–1924* (London and New York, 1988).

Schulkind, Jeanne (ed.), *Virginia Woolf, Moments of Being: Unpublished Autobiographical Writings* (London, 1976).

Woolf, Leonard (ed.), *A Writer's Diary, Being Extracts from the Diary of Virginia Woolf* (London and Toronto, 1953).

The rest of this bibliography is arranged to relate to each of the sections of the book, for ease of reference. Some items therefore appear more than once; the works of Virginia Woolf are not, however, repeated. Essays appearing in Beja's *Casebook* (1970) are cited with that reference.

Early Reviews

Beja, M. (ed.), *Virginia Woolf, To the Lighthouse, A Casebook* (London, 1970).

Majumdar, R. and McLaurin, A. (eds), *Virginia Woolf, The Critical Heritage* (London and Boston, Mass., 1975).

Virginia Woolf's Discussion of Modern Novels

Bennett, Arnold, 'Is the Novel Decaying?', *Cassell's Weekly* (28 March 1923); reprinted in Majumdar and McLaurin, 1975, pp. 112–14.
Bowlby, Rachel, *Virginia Woolf, Feminist Destinations* (New York and Oxford, 1988).
Majumdar, R. and McLaurin, A. (eds), *Virginia Woolf, The Critical Heritage* (London and Boston, Mass., 1975).
Minow-Pinkney, Makiko, *Virginia Woolf and the Problem of the Subject* (Brighton, 1987).
The dispute with Bennett is mentioned by numerous writers. It is described in some detail in the following, none of which, however, gives a full account:
Daugherty, Beth Rigel, 'The Whole Contention Between Mr Bennett and Mrs Woolf, Revisited', in E. K. Ginsberg and L. M. Gottlieb (eds), *Virginia Woolf, Centennial Essays* (Troy, NY, 1983).
Hynes, Samuel, 'The Whole Contention Between Mr Bennett and Mrs Woolf', *Novel* (Fall 1967).
Kettle, Arnold, in his *An Introduction to the English Novel*, Volume 2 (London, 1953).
Kreuz, Irving, 'Mr Bennett and Mrs Woolf', *Modern Fiction Studies* 8 (Summer 1962).

'What Does She Mean?': Criticism in Woolf's Lifetime

Beja, M. (ed.), *Virginia Woolf, To the Lighthouse, A Casebook* (London, 1970; 1987).
Bradbrook, M. C., 'Notes on the Style of Mrs Woolf', *Scrutiny* 1, 1 (May 1932), 33–8.
Burra, P., 'Virginia Woolf', *The Nineteenth Century* 115 (1934) 112–25.
Edgar, P., 'The Stream of Consciousness', in his *The Art of the Novel* (New York, 1933).
Empson, W., 'Virginia Woolf', in E. Rickwood (ed.), *Scrutinies, Volume II, By Various Authors* (London, 1931).

Forster, E. M., *Aspects of the Novel* (London, 1927; Harmondsworth, 1962).
Forster, E. M., 'The Early Novels of Virginia Woolf', *Abinger Harvest* (London, 1936; Harmondsworth, 1967), pp. 119–29.
Forster, E. M., 'Virginia Woolf', in his *Two Cheers for Democracy* (London, 1951; Harmondsworth, 1965).
Hawkins, E. W., 'The Stream of Consciousness Novel', *Atlantic Monthly* (September 1926), 357–60.
Holtby, W., *Virginia Woolf* (London, 1932; Folcroft, Pa, 1969).
Leavis, F. R., 'After *To the Lighthouse*', *Scrutiny* 10, 3 (January 1942), 295–8.
Leavis, Q. D., *Fiction and the Reading Public* (London, 1932; 1965).
Monroe, E., 'The Inception of Mrs Woolf's Art', *College English*, 2 (1940), 217–30.
Mortimer, R., 'Mrs Woolf and Mr Strachey', *American Bookman* 68 (1929), 625–9.
Muller, H. J., 'Virginia Woolf and Feminine Fiction': (1) *The Saturday Review of Literature* (6 February 1937), 3–4; (2) enlarged version in H. J. Muller, *Modern Fiction: A Study of Values* (New York, 1937) pp. 317–28; reprinted in M. Beja (ed.), *Critical Essays on Virginia Woolf* (Boston, Mass., 1985).
Nicolson, H., 'The Writing of Virginia Woolf', *Listener* (18 November 1931), 864.
Peel, R., 'Virginia Woolf', *New Criterion* 13 (1933), 78–96.
Roberts, J. H., 'Toward Virginia Woolf', *Virginia Quarterly Review* 10 (1934), 587–602.
Troy, W., 'Virginia Woolf and the Novel of Sensibility', in Beja, 1970, pp. 85–9.

'Where Does She Fit In?': Virginia Woolf in Literary Histories

Allen, W., *The English Novel: A Short Critical History* (London, 1954; Harmondsworth, 1958).
Allen, W., *Tradition and Dream: A Critical Survey of British and American Fiction from the 1920s to the Present Day* (London, 1964; Harmondsworth, 1965).

Auerbach, E., *Mimesis: The Representation of Reality in Western Literature* (Berne, 1946; English edn, New York, 1953).
Booth, W. C., *The Rhetoric of Fiction* (Chicago, London and Toronto, 1961).
Bradbrook, F. W., 'Virginia Woolf: The Theory and Practice of Fiction' (1961), in B. Ford (ed.), *The Pelican Guide to English Literature, Volume 7, The Modern Age* (Harmondsworth, 1961), pp. 257–69, and B. Ford (ed.), *The New Pelican Guide to English Literature, Volume 7, From James to Eliot* (Harmondsworth, 1983), pp. 342–55.
Bradbury, M., *Possibilities: Essays on the State of the Novel* (London, Oxford and New York, 1973).
Bradbury, M. and McFarlane, J. (eds), *Modernism 1890–1930* (Harmondsworth, 1976).
Fowler, R., *Linguistic Criticism* (Oxford and New York, 1986).
Kenner, H., *A Sinking Island: The Modern English Writers* (London, 1988).
Kettle, A., 'Virginia Woolf: *To the Lighthouse*', in *An Introduction to the English Novel, Volume 2, Henry James to the Present Day* (London, 1953).
Leech, G. N. and Short, M., *Style in Fiction, A Linguistic Introduction to English Fictional Prose* (London and New York, 1981).
Lodge, D., *The Modes of Modern Writing, Metaphor, Metonymy, and the Typology of Modern Literature* (London, 1977).
McHale, B., *Postmodernist Fiction* (New York and London, 1987).
Williams, R., *The English Novel, From Dickens to Lawrence* (London, 1970; paperback edn, 1974).

New Criticism and its Followers: Symbolic and Allegorical Readings

Apter, T. E., *Virginia Woolf, A Study of Her Novels* (London, 1979).
Bassoff, B., 'Tables in Trees: Realism in *To the Lighthouse*', *Studies in the Novel* 16, 4 (Winter 1984) 424–34.
Beja, M. (ed.), *Virginia Woolf, 'To the Lighthouse', A Casebook* (London, 1970; 1987).

Bennett, J., *Virginia Woolf: Her Art as a Novelist* (Cambridge 1945; revised edn, 1964).
Blackstone, B., *Virginia Woolf, A Commentary* (London, 1949; 1972).
Burra, P., 'Virginia Woolf', *The Nineteenth Century*, 115 (1934), 112–25.
Chambers, R. L., *The Novels of Virginia Woolf* (Edinburgh, 1947).
Cox, C. B., *The Free Spirit: A Study of Humanism in the Novels of George Eliot, Henry James, E. M. Forster, Virginia Woolf, Angus Wilson* (London, 1963).
Daiches, D., *The Novel and the Modern World* (Chicago, 1939).
Daiches, D., *Virginia Woolf* (London, 1945).
Dekoven, M., 'History as Suppressed Referent in Modernist Fiction', *ELH* (*English Literary History*) 51 (Spring 1984), 137–52.
Friedman, N., 'Double Vision in *To the Lighthouse* (1955), in Beja, 1970, pp. 149–68.
Gliserman, M., 'Virginia Woolf's *To the Lighthouse*: Syntax and the Female Centre', *American Imago* 40, 1 (1983), 51–101.
Gordon, L., *Virginia Woolf, A Writer's Life* (Oxford and London, 1984).
Graham, J., 'Time in the Novels of Virginia Woolf', *University of Toronto Quarterly* 18 (January 1949), 186–201.
Hafley, J., 'The Creative Modulation of Perspective' (1954), in Beja, 1970, pp. 133–48.
Kaehele, S., and German, H., '*To the Lighthouse*: Symbol and Vision' (1962), in Beja, 1970, pp. 189–209.
Kelley, A. van B., *The Novels of Virginia Woolf, Fact and Vision* (Chicago and London, 1973).
Kelley, A. van B., *To the Lighthouse, The Marriage of Life and Art* (Boston, Mass., 1987).
Leaska, M., *Virginia Woolf's Lighthouse, A Study in Critical Method* (London, 1970).
Leaska, M., *The Novels of Virginia Woolf, From Beginning to End* (London, 1977).
Lee, H., *The Novels of Virginia Woolf* (London, 1977).
Moody, A. D., *Virginia Woolf, Writers and Critics Series* (Edinburgh, 1963).
Paul. J., *The Victorian Heritage of Virginia Woolf, The External World in Her Novels* (Norman, Okla., 1987).

Pederson, G., 'Vision in *To the Lighthouse*', *PMLA* 73 (1958), 585–600.
Rosenthal, M., *Virginia Woolf* (London, 1979).
Stewart, J. F., 'Light in *To the Lighthouse*', *Twentieth Century Literature* (October 1977), 377–89.
Stoddart, H., *To the Lighthouse* (screenplay), directed C. Gregg, BBC TV Productions in association with Colin Gregg Films Ltd (1983).
Thakur, N. C., *The Symbolism of Virginia Woolf* (London, 1965).
Velicu, A., *Unifying Strategies in Virginia Woolf's Experimental Fiction* (Uppsala, 1985).

Mythological and Freudian Readings

Beja, M. (ed.), *Virginia Woolf, To the Lighthouse, A Casebook* (London, 1970; 1987).
Blotner, J. L., 'Mythic Patterns in *To the Lighthouse*' (1956), in Beja, 1970, pp. 169–88.
Chodorow, N., *The Reproduction of Mothering: Psychoanalysis and the Sociology of Gender* (Berkeley, Calif., 1978).
Corner, M., 'Mysticism and Atheism in *To the Lighthouse*', *Studies in the Novel* 13 (Winter 1981).
DiBattista, M., '*To the Lighthouse*, Virginia Woolf's Winter's Tale', Chapter 3 of her *Virginia Woolf's Major Novels: The Fables of Anon* (New Haven, Conn., and London, 1980); as separate essay in R. Freedman (ed.), *Virginia Woolf, Revaluation and Continuity* (Los Angeles and London, 1980).
Dick, S. (ed.), *Virginia Woolf: To the Lighthouse, The Original Holograph Draft* (Toronto, Buffalo and London, 1982).
Hoffman, A. G., 'Demeter and Poseidon: Fusion and Distance in *To the Lighthouse*', *Studies in the Novel* 16 (Summer 1984), 182–96.
Hussey, M., *The Singing of the Real World, The Philosophy of Virginia Woolf's Fiction* (Columbus, Ohio, 1986).
Lilienfeld, J., ' "The Deceptiveness of Beauty": Mother Love and Mother Hate in *To the Lighthouse*', *Twentieth Century Literature* 23, 3 (October 1977), 345–73.
Overcarsh, F. L., 'The Lighthouse, Face to Face', *Accent* X (Winter 1950), 107–23.

Pederson, G., 'Vision in *To the Lighthouse*', *PMLA* 73 (1958), 585–600.

Readings in Aesthetic Theory

Bell, C., *Art* (London, 1914).
Cohn, R., 'Art in *To the Lighthouse*', *Modern Fiction Studies* 8 (1962), 127–36.
Dowling, D., *Bloomsbury Aesthetics and the Novels of Forster and Woolf* (London, 1985).
Friedman, N., 'Double Vision in *To the Lighthouse* (1955), in Beja, 1970, pp. 149–68.
Fry, R., 'An Essay in Aesthetics', *New Quarterly* (1909); reprinted in his *Vision and Design*, pp. 22–39.
Fry, R., *Vision and Design* (1920).
Graham, J. W., 'A Negative Note on Bergson and Virginia Woolf', *Essays in Criticism* 6, i (1956), 70–4.
Johnstone, J. K., *The Bloomsbury Group: A Study of E. M. Forster, Virginia Woolf, Lytton Strachey, and their Circle* (London, 1954).
McLaurin, A., *Virginia Woolf, The Echoes Enslaved* (Cambridge, 1973).
Matro, T. G., 'Only Relations: Vision and Achievement in *To the Lighthouse*', *PMLA* 99, 2 (1984a), 212–24.
Matro, T. G., 'Reply', *PMLA* 99, 5 (1984b), 1,000–1.
May, K. M., 'The Symbol of "Painting" in Virginia Woolf's *To the Lighthouse*', *Review of English Literature* 8 (1967), 91–8.
Morris, J., *Time and Timelessness in Virginia Woolf* (Hicksville, NY, 1977).
Roberts, J. H., 'Vision and Design in Virginia Woolf', *PMLA* 61 (September 1946), 835–47.
Schneider, D., '*To the Lighthouse*', *PMLA* 99, 5 (1984), 999–1,000.
Whiteley, P. J., *Knowledge and Experimental Realism in Conrad, Lawrence, and Woolf* (Baton Rouge and London, 1987).

The Narrative Voice

Auerbach, E., *Mimesis: The Representation of Reality in Western Literature* (Berne, 1946; English edn, New York, 1953).

Burt, J., 'Irreconcilable Habits of Thought in *A Room of One's Own* and *To the Lighthouse*', *ELH* 49 (1982), 889–907; reprinted in Harold Bloom (ed.), *Virginia Woolf: Modern Critical Views* (New York, 1986), pp. 191–206.
Fleishman, A., *Virginia Woolf, A Critical Reading* (Baltimore, Md, and London, 1975).
Harper, H., *Between Language and Silence: The Novels of Virginia Woolf* (Baton Rouge and London, 1982).
Hartman, G., 'Virginia's Web', *Chicago Review* 14 (Spring 1961); reprinted in Harold Bloom (ed.), *Virginia Woolf: Modern Critical Views* (New York, 1986).
McLaughlin, T. M., 'Fiction and Interpretation in Virginia Woolf', *Essays in Literature* 8, 2 (Fall 1981), 173–87.
Mepham, J., 'Figures of Desire: Narration and Fiction in *To the Lighthouse*', in Gabriel Josipovici (ed.), *The Modern English Novel, the Reader, the Writer and the Work* (London, 1976), pp. 149–85.
Miller, J. H., 'Mr Carmichael and Lily Briscoe: The Rhythm of Creativity in *To the Lighthouse*', in R. Kiely with J. Hildebidle (eds), *Modernism Reconsidered* (Cambridge, Mass., and London, 1983).
Naremore, J., *The World Without a Self, Virginia Woolf and the Novel* (New Haven, Conn., and London, 1973).
Ruotolo, L. P., *The Interrupted Moment: A View of Virginia Woolf's Novels* (Stanford, Calif., 1986).

Virginia Woolf and Feminism

Burt, J., 'Irreconcilable Habits of Thought in *A Room of One's Own* and *To the Lighthouse*', *ELH* 49 (1982), 889–907; reprinted in Harold Bloom (ed.), *Virginia Woolf: Modern Critical Views* (New York, 1986), pp. 191–206.

Biographical Readings

Bazin, N. T., *Virginia Woolf and the Androgynous Vision* (New Jersey, 1973).
Beer, G., 'Hume, Stephen, and Elegy in *To the Lighthouse*', in her *Arguing With The Past: Essays in Narrative From Woolf to*

Sidney (1989), pp. 183–202; first published in *Essays in Criticism* 34 (1984).

Beja, M. (ed.), *Virginia Woolf, To the Lighthouse, A Casebook* (London, 1970; 1987).

Bell, Q., *Virginia Woolf, A Biography*, 2 volumes (London and New York, 1972).

Bicknell, J. W., 'Mr Ramsay was Young Once', in J. Marcus, 1987a, pp. 52–67.

DeSalvo, L., *Virginia Woolf: The Impact of Childhood Sexual Abuse on Her Life and Work* (Boston, Mass., 1989).

Ginsberg, E. K. and Gottlieb, L. M. (eds), *Virginia Woolf: Centennial Essays* (Troy, NY, 1983).

Gordon, L., *Virginia Woolf, A Writer's Life* (Oxford and London, 1984).

Gregor, I., 'Spaces: *To the Lighthouse*', in L. L. Martz and A. Williams (eds), *The Author in His Work, Essays on a Problem in Criticism* (New Haven, Conn., London, 1978), pp. 375–89.

Guiget, J., *Virginia Woolf and her Works* (1962), trans. J. Stewart (London 1965); 'To the Lighthouse', pp. 248–60, reprinted in Beja, 1970, pp. 231–45.

Heilbrun, C., *Towards Androgyny, Aspects of Male and Female in Literature* (New York and London, 1973), pp. 151–67 and 188–9; reprinted as 'Woolf and Androgyny', in Morris Beja (ed.), *Critical Essays on Virginia Woolf* (Boston, Mass., 1985), pp. 73–84.

Heilbrun, C., *Writing a Woman's Life* (New York, 1988; London, 1989).

Kahane, C., 'The Nuptials of Metaphor: Self and Other in Virginia Woolf', *Literature and Psychology* 30, 2 (1980), pp. 72–82.

Kennedy, R., *A Boy at the Hogarth Press* (London, 1972).

Lehmann, J., *Virginia Woolf* (London, 1975).

Love, J. O., *Virginia Woolf: Sources of Madness and Art* (Berkeley, Calif., 1977).

Marcus, J. (ed.), *New Feminist Essays on Virginia Woolf* (Lincoln, Nebr., and London, 1981).

Marcus, J. (ed.), *Virginia Woolf, A Feminist Slant* (Lincoln, Nebr., 1983).

Marcus, J. (ed.), *Virginia Woolf and Bloomsbury: A Centenary Celebration* (Indiana and London, 1987a).

Marcus, J., *Virginia Woolf and the Languages of Patriarchy* (Indiana, 1987b).
Marcus, J., *Art and Anger, Reading Like a Woman* (Columbus, Ohio, 1988).
Marder, H., *Feminism and Art: A Study of Virginia Woolf* (Chicago and London, 1968).
Noble, J. R. (ed.), *Recollections of Virginia Woolf* (London, 1972).
Panken, S., *Virginia Woolf and the 'Lust of Creation': A Psychoanalytic Exploration* (Albany, NY, 1987).
Poole, R., *The Unknown Virginia Woolf* (Cambridge, 1978).
Rose, P., *Woman of Letters: A Life of Virginia Woolf* (New York and London, 1978).
Ruddick, S., 'Learning to Live With the Angel in the House', *Women's Studies* 4 (1977), 181–200.
Spivak, G. C., 'Unmaking and Making in *To the Lighthouse*', in S. McConnell-Ginet, R. Borker and N. Furman (eds), *Women and Language in Literature and Society* (New York, 1980), pp. 310–27.
Trautmann, J., 'Introduction', in E. K. Ginsberg and L. M. Gottlieb (eds), *Virginia Woolf: Centennial Essays* (Troy, NY, 1983), pp. 1–10.
Trombley, S., *'All That Summer She Was Mad': Virginia Woolf and Her Doctors* (London, 1981).
Warner, E. (ed.), *Virginia Woolf: A Centenary Perspective* (London, 1984).
Woolf, L., *Sowing: An Autobiography of the Years 1880–1904* (London and New York, 1960).
Woolf, L., *Growing: An Autobiography of the Years 1904–11* (London, 1961; New York, 1962).
Woolf, L., *Beginning Again: An Autobiography of the Years 1911–18* (London and New York, 1964).
Woolf, L., *Downhill All the Way: An Autobiography of the Years 1919–39* (London and New York, 1967).
Woolf, L., *The Journey Not the Arrival Matters: An Autobiography of the Years 1939–69* (London, 1969; New York, 1970).

Theories of Femininity

Abel, E., '"Cam the Wicked": Woolf's Portrait of the Artist as her Father's Daughter', in J. Marcus, 1987a, pp. 170–94.
Bowlby, R., *Virginia Woolf: Feminist Destinations* (New York and Oxford, 1988).
Chodorow, N., 'Feminism and Difference: Gender, Relation, and Difference in Psychoanalytic Perspective' (1979), in M. R. Walsh (ed.), *The Psychology of Women, Ongoing Debates* (New Haven, Conn., and London, 1987), pp. 249–64.
Chodorow, N., *The Reproduction of Mothering: Psychoanalysis and the Sociology of Gender* (Berkeley, Calif., and London, 1978).
Haller, E., 'Isis Unveiled: Virginia Woolf's Use of Egyptian Myth', in J. Marcus, 1983, pp. 109–31.
Heilbrun, C., '*To the Lighthouse*: The New Story of Mother and Daughter', *ADE Bulletin* 87 (Fall 1987), 12–14.
Homans, M., *Bearing the Word, Language and Female Experience in Nineteenth-Century Writing* (Chicago and London, 1986).
Kristeva, J., *About Chinese Women* (1974a), relevant sections in T. Moi (ed.), 1986, pp. 138–59.
Kristeva, J., 'Revolution in Poetic Language' (1974b), in T. Moi (ed.), 1986, pp. 89–136.
Lidoff, J., 'Virginia Woolf's Feminine Sentence: The Mother-Daughter World of *To the Lighthouse*', *Literature and Psychology* 32, 3 (1986), 43–59.
Marcus, J. (ed.), *New Feminist Essays on Virginia Woolf* (Lincoln, Nebr., and London, 1981).
Marcus, J. (ed.), *Virginia Woolf: A Feminist Slant* (Lincoln, Nebr., 1983).
Marcus, J. (ed.), *Virginia Woolf and Bloomsbury: A Centenary Celebration* (Indiana and London, 1987a).
Marcus, J., *Virginia Woolf and the Languages of Patriarchy* (Indiana, 1987b).
Marcus, J., 'A Rose for Him to Rifle', in J. Marcus, 1987b, pp. 1–17.
Marcus, J., *Art and Anger, Reading Like a Woman* (Columbus, Ohio, 1988).
Marcus, J., 'Still Practice, A/Wrested Alphabet: Toward a Feminist Aesthetic', in J. Marcus, 1988, pp. 215–49.

Minow-Pinkney, M., *Virginia Woolf and the Problem of the Subject* (Brighton, 1987).
Moi, T., *Sexual/Textual Politics: Feminist Literary Theory* (London and New York, 1985).
Moi, T. (ed.), *The Kristeva Reader* (Oxford, 1986).
Millett, K., *Sexual Politics* (New York, 1970; London, 1971).
Mitchell, J., *Psychoanalysis and Feminism* (Harmondsworth, 1974).
Mitchell, J. and Rose, J. (eds), *Feminine Sexuality: Jacques Lacan and the Ecole Freudienne* (London, 1982).
Stubbs, P., *Women and Fiction: Feminism and the Novel 1880–1920* (London, 1979).
Todd, J., *Feminist Literary History: A Defence* (Cambridge, 1988).
Transue, P., *Virginia Woolf and the Politics of Style* (Albany, NY, 1986).
Waugh, P., *Feminine Fictions: Revisiting the Postmodern* (London, 1989).

Mrs Ramsay's Story

Lilienfeld, J., 'Where the Spear Plants Grew: the Ramsay's Marriage in *To the Lighthouse*', in J. Marcus, 1981, pp. 148–69.

Disintegration of Self

Kristeva, J., *About Chinese Women* (1974a), relevant sections in Moi, 1986, pp. 138–59.
Kristeva, J., 'Revolution in Poetic Language' (1974b), in Moi, 1986, pp. 89–136.
Kristeva, J., 'Women's Time' (1979) in Moi, 1986, pp. 187–213.
Marcus, J., 'A Rose for Him to Rifle', in J. Marcus, *Virginia Woolf and the Languages of Patriarchy* (Indiana, 1987b), pp. 1–17.
Moi, T. (ed.), *The Kristeva Reader* (Oxford, 1986).

The Narrative Voice Again

Auerbach, E., *Mimesis: The Representation of Reality in Western Literature* (Berne, 1946; English edn, New York, 1953).

Cameron, D., *Feminism and Linguistic Theory* (London, 1985).
Gilbert, S. M., 'Woman's Sentence, Man's Sentencing: Linguistic Fantasies in Woolf and Joyce', in J. Marcus (ed.), *Virginia Woolf and Bloomsbury, A Centenary Celebration* (Indiana and London, 1987a), pp. 208–24.
Gilbert, S. M. and Gubar, S., *No Man's Land, The Place of the Woman Writer in the Twentieth Century: Volume 1, The War of the Words* (New Haven, Conn., and London, 1988).
Gilbert, S. M. and Gubar, S., *The Madwoman in the Attic, The Woman Writer and the Nineteenth Century Imagination* (New Haven, Conn., and London, 1979).
Maitland, S. and Wandor, M., *Arky Types* (London, 1987).
Mepham, J., 'Figures of Desire: Narration and Fiction in *To the Lighthouse*', in Gabriel Josipovici (ed.), *The Modern English Novel, the Reader, the Writer and the Work* (London, 1976), pp. 149–85.
Miller, J. H., 'Mr Carmichael and Lily Briscoe: The Rhythm of Creativity in *To the Lighthouse*', in R. Kiely with J. Hildebidle (eds), *Modernism Reconsidered* (Cambridge, Mass., and London, 1983).
Minow-Pinkney, M., *Virginia Woolf and the Problem of the Subject* (Brighton, 1987).

Index

Abel, Elizabeth 69–70, 78, 98
Aiken, Conrad 9
allegorical readings 25–33
Allen, Walter 22
androgyny 37, 54, 60, 74
Apter, T. E. 32
art, in *To the Lighthouse* 29, 30, 32, 34, 39–43
Auerbach, Erich 18–21, 47, 49, 96
Austen, Jane 53
author, the, concepts of 11–12, 13, 19–21, 44–5
autobiography, *To the Lighthouse* read as 18, 33, 36, 55–65

Bankes, William 19, 28, 41, 82–3
Bassoff, Bruce 32
Bazin, Nancy Topping 60
Beer, Gillian 62–5
Beja, Morris (ed.), *Virginia Woolf, To the Lighthouse, A Casebook* 9, 16, 28–9, 60
Bell, Quentin 55–6, 58
Bennett, Arnold 11, 12, 16, 96
Bennett, Joan 26, 30
Bergson, Henri 16–17, 39
Bicknell, John W. 60
Blackstone, Bernard 28
Bloomsbury Group 20, 23, 38
Blotner, Joseph L. 34–5, 36
Booth, Wayne 23
Bowlby, Rachel 13, 67–8
Bradbrook, F. W. 22
Bradbrook, M. G. 14
Bradbury, Malcolm 20; and James McFarlane 22–3

Brewster, Dorothy 29
Briscoe, Lily; and androgyny 60, 74, 93; and Charles Tansley 82; and Mr Ramsay 41, 73; and Mrs Ramsay 37–8, 41–2, 62, 91, 93; and Mrs Ramsay's absence 27, 28, 31–2, 62, 73, 90; and the Ramsays' marriage 30, 35, 74; and Paul and Minta 85; and the 'semiotic' 90–1, 92; her question 21; her picture 22, 26, 29, 30, 31–2, 34, 36, 37, 40, 41–2, 49, 62, 73, 85, 90
Brontë, Charlotte 53
Burra, Peter 16, 30
Burt, John 44, 52

Cameron, Deborah 97
Carmichael, Augustus 37, 38, 49–50, 82, 88, 92
Casebook see 'Beja'
Chambers, R. L. 25
characters in fiction 9, 12–13, 14, 19–50
Chodorow, Nancy 37–8, 68–9, 72–3, 76–7
Christianity 27–8, 33–4, 64, 88
Cohn, Ruby 40
colour symbolism 26
Corner, Martin 34
Cox, C. B. 30
Critical Heritage, The see 'Majumdar'

Daiches, David 25–6, 27
Dekoven, Marianne 33

Demeter 34–8, 66
DeSalvo, Louise 65
DiBattista, Maria 36–7
Dick, Susan 37
Dis 34
Dowling, David 42–3
Doyle, Minta (and Paul Rayley) 82, 85

Edgar, P. 17
Empson, William 15–16

femininity (see also 'androgyny', 'Chodorow', 'Kristeva', 'Lacan', 'Oedipus Complex', 'women and writing'); and death 35, 85, 86, 91; as destructive 36, 37–8, 68–9, 76; as nurturing 27, 32, 35–6, 60, 68, 80–5; as silence 69–72, 75, 97–8; as stupidity 68, 97; females as object 67–8, 72; females as subject 69–78; in mythology 35–8, 66; phallus, non-possession of 71–2; pre-Oedipal state 67, 68–9, 73, 74, 76, 86–90; 'semiotic', the 74–5, 77–8, 86–92, 96–7; social experience of women, relevance of 33, 66, 75–6, 80–5; stereotypes 27, 28, 54, 74–5, 92–3, 97
Feminist criticism 29, 33, 34, 36, 52–78, 79–98
First World War 33, 49
Fleishman, Avrom 43
form of *To the Lighthouse* 9–10, 14–18, 38–43, 43–51, 91–8
Forster, E. M. 15
Fowler, Roger 23
free indirect discourse 48
Freud (see also 'Oedipus Complex') 34, 35, 66, 68, 70–1, 73, 76, 92
Friedman, Norman 29, 30, 43
Fry, Roger 32, 39–43

Gilbert, Sandra, and Susan Gubar 97, 98

Ginsberg, E. K., and L. M. Gottlieb 59
Gliserman, M. 32
Gordon, Lyndall 33, 57
Graham, J. 30
Graham, J. W. 39
Gregor, Ian 61
Guiget, Jean 61

Hafley, James 28–9, 30
Harper, Howard 44
Hartman, Geoffrey 48–9
Harvey, John 60
Hawkins, E. W. 17
Heilbrun, Carolyn 59, 60–1, 69
Hoffman, Anne G. 37
Holtby, Winifred 14, 17
Homans, Margaret 76–8
Hussey, Mark 34

Isis 66

Johnstone, J. K. 38
Jung 34

Kaehele, Sharon, and Howard German 29, 30
Kahane, Claire 59
Kelley, Alice van Buren 29–31
Kennedy, Richard 57
Kenner, Hugh 24
Kettle, Arnold 23
Kristeva, Julia 73–6, 85–93, 96–7
Kronenberger, Louis 9

Lacan, Jacques 65, 71–2, 73, 74, 76–7, 97
Leaska, Michael 26–7, 36
Leavis, F. R. 18, 60
Leavis, Q. D. 14
Lee, Hermione 31–2
Leech, G., and Short, M. 23
Lehmann, John 57
Lidoff, Joan 69
'life', in fiction 11, 13, 14–16, 18
lighthouse, alleged symbolism of 16, 26–7, 28, 29, 30, 32, 33, 35, 37

'Lighthouse, The' 21, 28, 29, 30, 36, 37, 42, 46–7, 62, 70, 91–2
Lilienfeld, Jane 38, 80
Linguistic Criticism 23, 45–51, 93–8
Lodge, David 20–1, 22
Love, Jean O. 57

McHale, Brian 21
McLaughlin, T. M. 43–4
McLaurin, Allen (see also 'Majumdar') 9, 12–13, 40–1
McNab, Mrs 31, 50, 75, 91, 92
Maitland, Sara and Michelene Wandor 97
Majumdar, Robin, and Allen McLaurin (eds), *Virgina Woolf, The Critical Heritage* 9, 12–13
Marcus, Jane 57–8, 75–6, 91, 98
Marxist Criticism 23
masculinity (see also 'androgyny', 'Lacan', 'Oedipus Complex'); phallus, possession of 71–2; stereotypes 27, 28, 54, 74–5, 92–3, 97; the 'symbolic order' 74–5, 76–8, 86–92, 96–7
Matro, Thomas G. 41–2
May, Keith M. 40
Mepham, John 45–8, 49, 91, 93, 96
metaphor and metonymy 21, 46–7
Miller, J. Hillis 45, 48–51, 62, 93
Millett, Kate 66
minor writer, Woolf described as 22–4
Minow-Pinkney, Makiko 13, 74–5, 96
Mitchell, Juliet 67, 71–2
modernism 10–11, 19–23, 44, 93–6
Moers, Ellen 66
Moi, Toril 73–4, 75, 92–3
Monroe, Elizabeth 15, 17
Moody, A. D. 29
Moore, G. E. 38
Morris, Jill 39
Mortimer, Raymond 18
Muir, Edwin 9

Muller, Herbert J. 18
Myth Criticism 33–8

Naremore, James 44–5
narration of *To the Lighthouse* 13, 19–20, 43–51, 93–8
New Criticism 25–33
Nicolson, Harold 15
Noble, Joan Russell 57

Oedipus Complex 35–8, 67–78, 85–93
Overcarsh, F. L. 33–4

Panken, Shirley 59
Paul, Janis 32
Pederson, Glenn 27, 30, 36
Peel, Robert 15
Persephone 34–8, 66
plot, alleged absence of in *To the Lighthouse* 10, 16, 18, 22, 28, 32, 39, 72
poetry, the novel as 9–10, 14–16, 22, 26
Poole, Roger 56–7, 59
Poseidon 37

Ramsay, Cam; and masculine power in language 69–70, 85, 98; and the 'semiotic' 77–8; as a child 69, 77, 83; elided with James 28, 30, 32, 36, 49, 60
Ramsay, James; as a child 19, 83, 86, 94–6; Oedipal experience 35, 36–8, 42, 67, 70, 92; opening scenes of the novel, narration of 19, 94–6; voyage to the lighthouse 22, 28, 30, 32, 35, 36, 49, 60, 70
Ramsay, Mr; and Lily 26, 32, 41, 73; and James 35, 36–7, 60; and Leslie Stephen 18, 59, 60, 62–5; and Mrs Ramsay 27, 28, 29, 30, 31, 33, 36, 38, 49, 60, 67–8, 83–5, 86; and Mrs Ramsay's absence 62; and philosophy 27, 43, 62–5; and the 'symbolic order' 86, 88–92;

Ramsay, Mr; and Lily — *continued*
  at the lighthouse 31, 32, 34, 35, 60; comic 28, 67; opening scene, narrative dislike in 95–6
Ramsay, Mrs; as an absence 28, 31-2, 37–8, 62, 73, 92; as an object 68; as 'angel in the house' 80–5; as mother-figure 28, 30, 32, 35–8, 42, 60–1; as a symbol 16, 26, 27–8, 29, 30, 32, 33–4; as Demeter/Persephone 34–8; as Victorian 44; and death 49, 85, 91; and Julia Stephen 59; and James 36–7, 60, 81; and men 80–5; and Lily 35, 37–8, 42, 68; and Mr Ramsay 28, 34–6, 60, 81–5, 88–90; and the narrative voice 19; and the 'semiotic' 85–91; critics hostile to 27, 30, 36; domestic creativity 49; her dinner-party 40, 42; her 'triumph' 82–3, 84, 87; 'wedge-shaped core of darkness' 40, 83–4, 86–8
Rayley, Paul (and Minta Doyle) 82, 85
reader, the experience of the 10, 11, 13–14, 16, 42–5, 66, 90–3, 93–7
representation, fiction as 9–10, 11–13, 14–18, 21, 34, 39–43, 62
Roberts, John Hawley 14, 16, 17, 39–40
Rose, Phyllis 57, 59
Rosenthal, Michael 32
Ruddick, Sara 59
Ruotolo, L. P. 44

Schneider, Daniel J. 42
sea, alleged symbolism of 28, 29, 30, 31
'semiotic', the 74–8, 85–92, 96–7
Scrutiny 14, 18
Spivak, Gayatri C. 61–2
St Ives 33
Stephen, Sir Leslie 18, 36, 59, 60, 62–5

Stewart, Jack F. 32
Stoddart, Hugh, and Colin Gregg 33
'stream of consciousness' (see also 'free indirect discourse') 17, 20
symbolic readings 16, 22, 25–33
'symbolic order', the 65, 70–8, 85–92

Tansley, Charles 33, 34, 67, 82
television film of *To the Lighthouse* 33
Thakur, N. C. 27–8
'Time Passes' 9, 26, 28, 29, 30, 31, 33, 35, 36, 37, 48, 50, 61, 62, 91
Times Literary Supplement 9, 11
Todd, Janet 75
Transue, Pamela 66
Trautmann, Joanne 58–9
Trombley, Stephen 57
Troy, William 16–17

Velicu, A. 32

Warner, E. 60
Waugh, Patricia 72–3
Whiteley, Patrick J. 43
Williams, Orlo 9
Williams, Raymond 23
'Window, The' 18–19, 28, 30, 31, 36, 37, 46–7, 62, 69, 80–5, 91
women and writing 13, 53–5, 56–9, 65, 69–70, 85, 97–8
Woolf, Leonard 12–13, 55–6, 59
Woolf, Virgina, other works: *Between the Acts* 66; *The Common Reader* 10; *Diary* 29, 56; *Jacob's Room* 12; *Letters* 32–33, 56, 59; 'Modern Fiction' 10, 11, 13, 17, 18; 'Modern Novels' 11–12, 13, 17, 20, 96; *Moments of Being* 56, 59; 'Mr Bennett and Mrs Brown' (first version) 12; *Mr Bennett and Mrs Brown* ('Character in Fiction') 10, 11, 13; *Mrs Dalloway* 39, 66; *Orlando* 53, 81; 'Professions for Women' 80; *A Room of One's Own* 13, 33, 44, 52–5, 58, 66, 81, 97, 98; *Three Guineas* 66; *The Waves* 22